AF072346

The

# Southern Way

The regular volume for the Southern devotee

**Kevin Robertson**

## Issue 54

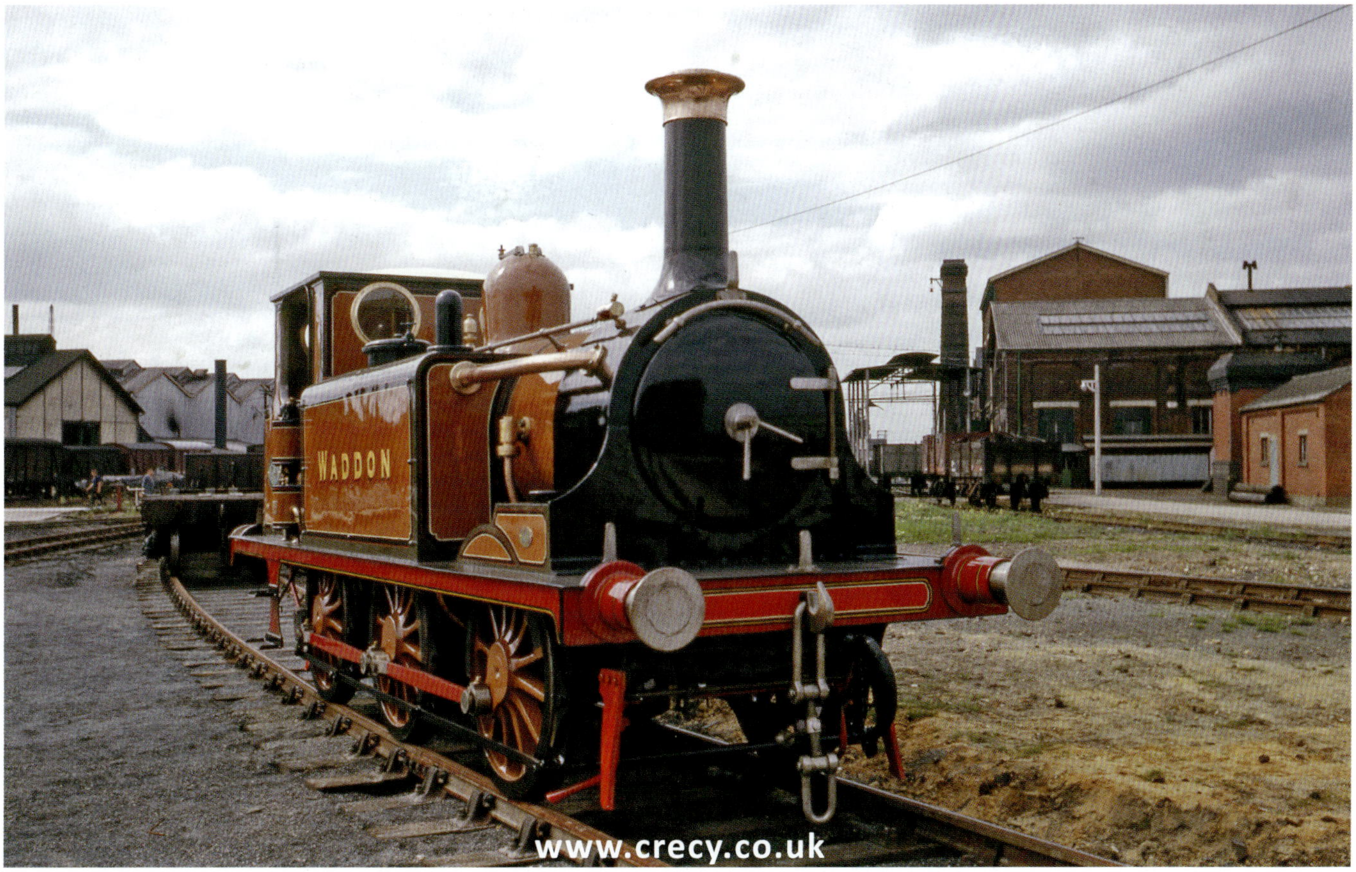
WADDON
www.crecy.co.uk

© 2021 Crécy Publishing Ltd
and the various contributors

ISBN 9781800350236

First published in 2021 by Noodle Books
an imprint of Crécy Publishing Ltd

**New contact details**
**All editorial submissions to:**
The Southern Way (Kevin Robertson)
**'Silmaril'**
**Upper Lambourn**
**Hungerford**
**Berkshire RG17 8QR**
Tel: 01488 674143
editorial@thesouthernway.co.uk

All rights reserved. No part of this book may be reproduced or transmitted in any form or by any means electronic or mechanical, including photocopying, recording or by any information storage without permission from the Publisher in writing. All enquiries should be directed to the Publisher.

A CIP record for this book is available from the British Library

Publisher's note: Every effort has been made to identify and correctly attribute photographic credits. Any error that may have occurred is entirely unintentional.

Printed in the UK by Cambrian Printers Ltd

**Noodle Books is an imprint of**
**Crécy Publishing Limited**
1a Ringway Trading Estate
Shadowmoss Road
Manchester M22 5LH

**www.crecy.co.uk**

*Front cover:*
4-COR unit No. 3123 on a Coastway service at Hove. These were some of the last workings for what had once been the family of 4-COR/4-RES/4-BUF/4iGRI and 4-COR(N) sets before final withdrawal in 1972. Unit 3123 (BR Class designation '404') had been one of the original units built for the Portsmouth electrification in 1937. In the opinion of the writer, green was the colour that suited them best, corporate blue/grey almost seeming to emphasise the aged pre-war styling in exactly the same way as it appeared on the 'Brighton Belle' Pullman. One four-car set, No. 3142, is preserved although not in (electric) running order. What may not be widely known is that continuing the SR tradition of re-use, upon withdrawal the bodies were scrapped but several of the coach underframes were reused by the Chief Civil Engineer's department as carriers for long welded rail and also as crane runners. *Graham Smith*

*Rear cover:*
Lest we be accused of foregoing steam, here we have No. 35030 *Elder Dempster Lines* powering through Woking with the Down 'Atlantic Coast Express'. Under this name, the train first ran on 19 July 1926, continuing to do so as a through service to the various coastal resorts of Devon and Cornwall served by the Southern until each was 'pruned' by Dr Beeching from 1964 onwards. The name of the train was revived by the privatised First Great Western in 2008 and continues to serve Bude, at least albeit by a bus connection from Exeter St. Davids.

*Title page:*
*Waddon* beautifully restored for preservation in Montreal, circa October 1963. Originating of course from the LBSCR works at Brighton in 1875, No. 54, as she was then identified, was sold to the SECR in September 1904 becoming their No. 751. Under combined Southern Railway ownership she became No. 680, and was of the type later engaged in shunting at Lancing Carriage Works. Restored to LBSCR livery the engine was shipped to the Canadian Railway Museum at Montreal where she remains. *S. C. Townroe*

# Contents

**Issue No 55 of THE SOUTHERN WAY**
**ISBN 9781800350267**
**available in July 2021 at £14.95**

To receive your copy the moment it is released, order in advance from your usual supplier, or it can be sent post-free (UK) direct from the publisher:

Crécy Publishing Ltd (Noodle Books)
1a Ringway Trading Estate, Shadowmoss Road, Manchester M22 5LH
Tel 0161 499 0024
www.crecy.co.uk
enquiries@crecy.co.uk

Introduction ............................................................. 4

The S. C. Townroe Archive – in Colour ................... 5
   Part 3

The South Western and the Variable ................... 14
   Vortex Blastpipe

Down to Earth Part 3B ........................................... 17
   Ex-LBSCR Stock

Spotting on the Somerset & Dorset ..................... 22
   Bill Allen

The Railways of the Wandle Valley ....................... 26
   Part 2

John Gaywood Click ............................................... 33
   'Engineering the Southern' Part 5

The Colour of the Southern .................................. 44

Southern Staff ........................................................ 50

Stored Engines ....................................................... 52

Rebuilt ..................................................................... 64
   The Letters and Comments Pages

Horse Power on the Hampton Court Branch
   in 1849 ............................................................... 71
   David Turner

The Raynes Park Derailment ................................ 73
   28 November 1967
   Peter Tatlow

The Long Lost Shirley Holms Halt ........................ 78
   Roger Simmonds

A Very Brief Visit to Newhaven – June 1952 ........ 80
   Courtesy Gerry Nichols and
   the Stephenson Locomotive Society

Architecture and Imagery on the Cuckoo Line ..... 82

Looking Back… ....................................................... 88

Errata – In More Ways Than One! ....................... 95

# Introduction

Regular readers will be aware that necessary scheduling of *Southern Way* means there is the need to have an issue in preparation the month prior to the preceding one appearing. Consequently for this April issue I am starting to write this in December (and in March I will be starting on the July issue, etc, etc). The reasons for this lead time are both commercial and personal.

However, what this means in practice is that it can be very difficult to be topical – even in a basically historic journal – when faced with preparing something which will be at least four months out of date should I start to discuss current topics. At present too, that can hardly be avoided, Covid rages all around and I suspect that like me, many of you are even wary about stepping outside the door. Our age is against us. Consequently may I simply say I do hope all will have come through this tempest and 2021 may once again bring us the opportunity to pursue our leisure interests, which I trust will include a majority of rail-related journeys and visits, etc.

So as this is meant to be a publication dealing with history let us go back to history, and remember that history is not just ten, twenty, or a hundred years ago, it is yesterday, last week and last month.

I have a friend who is currently employed by one of the railway operators, tasked with getting some new trains into service. Hopefully, he and his colleagues will succeed as from the stories he tells of the trials and tribulations of doors, interlocks, p.a. announcements, and shut-downs, it does make me wonder if we have not just made things a bit over-complicated for the task required. The same as the new washing machine that arrived at 'SW headquarters' the other day. According to the manual it can be remotely programmed from your phone. But put simply, 'Why would I want to?' I (we) want it to wash clothes – as simple as that. The same as these new trains. If doors and the rest work perfectly on an existing design why not simply copy the same technology and avoid complications?

No doubt if I cared to search the web, YouTube and whatever Facebook group, I would find images galore of those who seem to record every last movement of whatever new train is on test. But it was certainly not so in the past. What we seem to have missed photographic-wise are images recording tests, trials (with the exception of the 1948 interchange workings), rebuildings, etc, relative to both infrastructure and new rolling stock and locomotives. How many images for example have you seen of locomotives on trial from Ashford, Brighton, or Eastleigh? How many images of station or junction remodelling at St. Mary Cray, Brighton, or Templecombe – and by this I am not necessarily referring to the few official views that might exist of some occasions, but those taken either by chance or by those 'in the know'.

Yes, some do exist and we must indeed be grateful, but even allowing for the paucity of film that has existed at certain times in our history and the issues of processing said product – a procedure the current generation would only laugh at – it just goes to indicate yet again not every area of railway history is covered.

Regular readers will be aware that I have spoken time and time again over the importance of securing one's own collection for posterity. Too much has been lost, not necessarily deliberately, but instead by unintended ignorance on the part of those who follow. Accordingly, it is with pleasure that I can report some good news concerning the name of P. M. Alexander. I had considered that this individual's collection of Southern material had disappeared forever. (There was an album featuring some of his WR images published by Wild Swan in 1983.) The good news is that the Lens of Sutton Association have custody of some 4,000 negatives (out of how many we do not know) from the collection. These are being sorted and listed and will one day, soon we hope, be available again. I know that like me, we can all look forward to accessing some fascinating views from decades past (not necessarily all Southern of course) but who knows, perhaps even some of my missing connections may even be included.

Kevin Robertson

**Compared with what might have been seen around the same time at the front of works – see frontispiece image of *Waddon* – a sad end to a magnificent machine. The death throes of a 'Schools' outside the rear of Eastleigh circa October 1963. No details as to the engine.** *S. C. Townroe*

# The S. C. Townroe Archive – in Colour
## Part 3

For this latest compilation we are focussing on just two locations, Eastleigh, Reading (Southern of course) and then back to Eastleigh again. No passenger trains either, just locomotives and a couple of derailments.

I suspect that like all, if the boss turned up the men would be on their toes, but most would anyway as a matter of course. Safety and procedures which had been built up over decades allied to an intimate knowledge of the rule book would, where necessary, immediately come into play. Indeed this almost literal application of rules and regulations might even be seen as the forerunner of today's modern Health & Safety regulations. To be fair H&S has gone a lot further; one cringes for example at the amount of asbestos used for insulation seen in the open; especially relative to the engines in varying stages of dismantling which we have in this issue.

Every one of the images in the SCT archive is similarly representative of a past age – a time which the modern railway sometimes seems to want to conveniently ignore and yet which laid the foundation for the network we have today. None of the items depicted may be running around on the rails of the network today, but each remains an essential component of the railway system of yesterday.

*Copies of the SCT scans – but only as they appear – are available for private or commercial use. Please enquire at editorial@thesouthernway.co.uk Watch this space also for details of something else very special planned for 2021.*

**The last Drummond S11 4-4-0 No. 30400 at Eastleigh shortly before being withdrawn in November 1954. There were just ten engines in this class of 4-4-0s which in their later years could sometimes be found working Lymington boat trains, a duty they shared with another LSWR design, the D15 class. Perhaps even regarded as a bit of a celebrity engine at its home shed of Guildford (from 1951), it somehow managed to survive three years beyond the cull of its nine sisters in 1951. (SCT cannot have had a lot of room to play with when taking this image as the buffer beam and almost the top of the chimney are cut off on the original slide.)**

Another BR (S) engine was No. 42098 which emerged from Brighton Works in July 1950 and remained on the Southern Region until January 1960. The Southern Region had been desperately in need of a modern large passenger tank engine even before nationalisation but memories of the Sevenoaks disaster haunted the corridors of Waterloo and as a result it was not until BR days that the Fairburn, Ivatt and, soon after, BR Standard designs began to appear. The original intention had been to number these engines allowed to BR in the 38xxx series but in the end as they were to an LMR design, it was decided that that region's numbering would be followed. No. 42098 is seen here at the Eastleigh coaling stage sometime in 1952, presumably a works visit or special working as she was at the time based at Ashford.

We might even entitle this as 'No slacking whilst the boss is about!' As replacement for many of the Drummond 4-4-0 types came the BR Standard 2-6-0 design in the 76xxx series, and from speaking to former Eastleigh men, it was generally liked as well. Here a brand new example, No. 76017, is receiving attention from the cleaners inside the shed, when at most six months old. No. 76017 would come to grief the very next year, 1954, when it lost control of its freight train descending the gradient into Whitchurch Town station. It was recovered, repaired and lasted until July 1965 and is now preserved on the Mid Hants Railway.

*Left and opposite page:*
The rebuilding of No. 35014 *Nederland Line* at Eastleigh in July 1956. This was one of the early rebuilds of the type organised on the simple basis of when a works overhaul was due together with available works capacity. Following this visit the engine was allocated to Nine Elms until September 1964 and then spent its final two and half years at Weymouth.

The S. C. Townroe Archive – in Colour

*Above and opposite page:* **Something slightly wrong at Reading** – no date but possibly around 1954. S15 No. 30834 has somehow managed to derail its rear driving wheels, fortunately with another set of rails alongside on to which the crane will be able to be positioned. As is often the case, it is difficult to identify the home depot of the crane with any certainty not being able to read the wording on the side with total certainty. Equally, why would SCT have been at Reading in the first place? This might tend to suggest it was the Eastleigh crane that was in attendance – Reading did not have its own crane – although it can be seen the local fitting staff here have already prepared as much as possible with wooden packing visible. Somehow the riding vans look slightly wrong for the Eastleigh crane so could this have been either the Guildford or Nine Elms example? Upon the crane's arrival behind No. 34009 *Lyme Regis*, we might find another clue as this was a Nine Elms-based engine throughout the 1950s. So is it the Nine Elms crane that has arrived? Whatever, we also see the re-railing in progress, watched no doubt with a little amusement by trains passing on the GW line above. Did Reading WR shed not have a crane it might have been possible to use…?

Back at Eastleigh we visit the scrapyard at the rear of the Works. What the Bulleid tender body is doing there is not certain, possibly scrap too as this was starting to get late in the day for steam, October 1963, although the early BR crest will also be noted. No. 32635 had been one of the Brighton Works shunters, hence the pseudo-LBSCR livery soon to be consigned to history. From the position of the Bulleid tender body ahead, this engine was probably in the same line up as the 'Schools' seen earlier.

The S. C. Townroe Archive – in Colour

A few years earlier in 1949 SCT recorded the remains of genuine faded LBSCR livery on another 'Terrier' also awaiting its turn for scrap and, from the corrosion visible, one that had also stood for some time. We are not given any details of individual locomotive identification. Don't think the bunker would be of much practical use…

Some engines were also dismantled within the works at Eastleigh, no doubt making the task a little easier than battling the elements (1955). This certainly does look more of a dismantling rather than a cutting exercise although the latter will no doubt follow at some stage. What we are seeing is probably the last image taken of 'E1/R' 0-6-2T No. 32094 formerly of Barnstaple Junction and Plymouth Friary. The work these engines performed had been taken over by newer and more powerful Ivatt 2-6-2T types.

Another ex-LBSCR type that met its end at Eastleigh was this former 4-6-0 rebuild, No. 32328. This was one of the 'Remembrance' class engines which had started its life as a tank engine. Seen here is the former *Hackworth,* its boiler seemingly lifted clear whilst the front end of the frames have already been removed. The nameplate support remains, for the moment at least, *in situ*. In the background are open wagons whose purpose was probably to cart away the pieces of metal once they had been reduced in size. Also seen is the rear of Eastleigh South signal box on the line between Eastleigh and Botley.

*Below and opposite page:* In May 1960 SCT was on hand to witness the result of a shunting incident in Eastleigh South yard in May 1960 involving a diesel shunter and what someone else might have referred to as 'troublesome trucks'. The diesel has stopped, deliberately or otherwise, close to the buffers (or perhaps even rebounded if the damage to the buffers was not new) with the following wagons failing to do likewise – the result was a typical case of buffer lock. There were several solutions to this type of situation, one being the removal of a buffer so allowing the other buffer to become detached from the entanglement. In this case the vehicles were judged to have been too closely connected and recourse was made instead to first removing as much of the train as possible before the crane arrived from the nearby shed to clear the final two wagons and so free the engine. After this would come the 'Please Explain' requests from various officials.

Next time: More bits broken off engines; some tank and tender engines; and the first of some branch line scenes.

13

# The South Western and the Variable Vortex Blastpipe

A recent find amongst a collection of miscellaneous items was a four-page record on the above covering the period 1890 to 1894.

We have no idea as to its origins. It is in typed form and with various abbreviations as to signatories, likely to have been works or running inspectors. As is so often the case when part of what was clearly a larger document is found, there are gaps in the information available. We can therefore do no more than commend it to readers for interest's sake if nothing else, with the suggestion that reference is also made to the Barry Curl and D. L .Bradley books on South Western Locomotive history.

One point that does come out is that towards the end of the 19th century locomotive testing was very much based on a 'trial and error' scenario. Advances were of course made later with the advent of the dynamometer car and controlled road testing but 'trial and error' would remain at the forefront of much steam locomotive testing almost to the end of steam itself.

Engine No. 534. August 1890. 'A12' class.

When this engine commenced running, the annulus could be reduced from 1" opening to ¼", but when used at the latter position, the blast (on the fire) was so great, and so many sparks were thrown out of the chimney, that it was thought advisable, with Mr A's (sen) sanction, to make ⅝" the minimum: which was accordingly done, and it was found that with stopping trains, when starting away from stations, that the annular space could be increased to its max. extent, and when this was done the pull on the fire was reduced to a min:, although with long runs without stopping it was found that the average opening varied between ⅜" and 11/16". It may be confidently said that if the apparatus is worked properly a great saving in fuel will be the result, and at a later date it is intended to run this engine against a similar one doing the same duties but not fitted with the variable opening.

On the 21 August it was found that the apparatus was not working, and on examination it was found that the spindle inside the smoke-boxsmokebox and carried by the lugs cast on the blastpipe, owing no doubt to the heat, and grit, had got jammed, and was almost immovable. With considerable difficulty this was released, and on another journey to Bournemouth the annulus was worked wide open for the greater part of the journey. When the smokebox was opened at the end of the journey a very small quantity of ashes were

**LSWR A12 No. 538, a sister engine to No. 534 described in the text.**

found and these of the finest quality. It is advisable that all the movable parts, especially in the smokebox, should be made a very easy fit (say 1/16" play) or a great deal of trouble will be experienced. Another bracket is also required to carry the rod outside the boiler. The average consumption of fuel for the three weeks the engine has been running is just under 27lbs per mile, but the engine being only just out of shops, and working very heavy trains, this amount can no doubt be still further reduced.

**Engine No. 453. October 1890. '445' class.**
Stated to work very easily, but owing to the smokebox drawing air on both sides, it has not up to the present time had a fair chance, and the smokebox has today had some cement put round the bottom of the exhaust pipe.

With stopping trains the annular orifice can be opened to its fullest extent, viz. 1"; and when this is done the blast on the fire is very little, but when long runs are made without a stop, it varies from 13/16" (18.66) to 5/8" (14.72) according to how the engine may be steaming. The ashes deposited in the smoke-box are of the finest quality and a marvellously small quantity even after working the engine heavily, and few if any sparks are thrown from the chimney. Up to the present time all the bearings, etc. connected with the apparatus, have given no trouble whatever, the working centres which have been adopted being a great improvement. I have no hesitation in saying that in the event of our adopting this form of blastpipe for all our engines there will be a great saving of fuel, and this will be specially noticeable in the case of suburban tank engines where the loads are heavy and the stops frequent, and the annular space can be kept wide open. (H.A.)

**Engine No. 534. October 1890. 'A12' class.**
No. 534, an engine fitted with a similar blastpipe, is doing remarkably well with regard to consumption, running on an average of about 26lbs per mile or 2lbs under the allowance.

Engine No. 560. September 1891. 'T3' class.
Engine resumed working 24/9/91. Travelled with and considered this form of variable top to be a very good one, both for simplicity and strength, and can be regulated without the slightest difficulty from the footplate, and if done so properly, the Engine will show an economy as regards coal consumption. The only fault to be found at present is its slack fit in the blastpipe which allows the steam to blow all round the outside of the cap, and strike the smokebox at various places, and I recommend that a larger cap be fitted. On the 1.55 up Bournemouth express the cap was not worked below ¾" opening which gives an annular area of 16.5 and shows a greater area by 2.59", compared with the old blastpipe. The cap can be regulated from ⅝" – 1" or from 13.99"-21.21". On travelling with this engine 19/10/91 the variable cap worked satisfactorily. (S.A.)

*Note: As mentioned, the information in this piece is copied verbatim from the original including where there is a mixture of imperial, decimal and sometimes nothing to indicate which form of measurement is being used. The provision of a drawing would have helped considerably.*

**Engine No. 580. October 1891. 'X2' class.**
Travelled with 30/10/91 by the 9.5am train from Waterloo. Two minutes late starting and another two minutes were lost owing to traffic delays, this time could easily have been made up if necessary. This train stops at Surbiton, Woking, Basingstoke, Whitchurch, Andover & Salisbury. At each of the places stopped at, the variable blastpipe was screwed to its full opening or 1", then after the engine had got away with the valves linked up to a cut-off of 28% the variable pipe was adjusted to an opening of 13/16" in the position the engine steamed best. A blastpipe opening of 1" gives an area of 21.21

*Below and overleaf:* **An LSWR X2 4-4-0 in photographic grey and in service.**

or an increase of 52%, over the least opening of ⅝" or an area of 13.99 sq. inches. But the working opening of the variable pipe was 13/16" or an area of 17.71. The fixed vortex pipe with a 5" gas pipe had an Opening for exhaust of 11/16" or an area of 13.91" so that the gain by the use of the variable pipe is 28% increase of area.

At Salisbury the working of the blastpipe was particularly examined. A new cap practically steam tight has been fitted, the whole of the exhaust being delivered fairly up the centre of the chimney, the gear for working the cap works freely in all positions and shows no signs of sticking. The average valve cut-off was 28%, below which the driver does not think it advisable to go; at this cut off in his opinion the engine works better, etc. The average boiler pressure was 160lbs. no great effort was made to maintain steam at 175lbs. The coal used was a poor, soft kind, about 25% being slack. With better fuel much better results could have been got both with regard to an increase in the blast opening and also to the steaming of the engine. (S. R. Sisterson)

**Engine No. 580. August 1892. 'X2' class.**
Recommended that this pipe be replaced by an ordinary 5" vortex pipe, owing to a very high consumption of coal, and that it may be tried on engines burning less coal than this one. (S.A.)

**Engine No. 586. April 1892. 'X2' class.**
After travelling several times on this engine I feel confident that the Variable Blastpipe is a great success. The Variable cap is used according to the quality of the coal supplied, for instance, with moderately good coal the engine will steam with ¾" width of annulus, and with exceptionally good coal a still larger annulus, while when the cap is right down, the engine will steam fairly well with the worst of coal. The engine will steam with good coal and a good white fire with the cap wide open for some distance, which I consider is a great advantage, as for instance, running from Basingstoke to Southampton West, a distance of 31 miles with the cap wide open a full pressure was maintained nearly all the way. I cannot at present suggest any alteration and believe this form of Pipe to be the best. (S.A.)

**Engine No. 586. March 1894. 'X2' class.**
This engine, No. 586, was reported 20/2/94 by Running Dept. for bad steaming owing to the Variable Blastpipe and they recommended the pipe be removed and a plain one substituted. I examined the blastpipe of the above engine and found the Levers and Eyebolts, which are of wrought iron, to be in bad condition, the slackness in the eyes being ⅝", owing to the wear and corrosion of the metal. The pipe was last refitted on the 22/6/93, and has been running up to the time it was taken out 26/2/94, the total mileage for the 8 months being 37,280. Until further experiments have been made I do not consider it advisable to refit any more Variable Blastpipes for Express Engines. (S.A.)

**Engines No. 596 & 594. April 1894. 'X2' class.**
The ordinary Vortex Blastpipes were substituted for the Variable ones on these engines on the 22 and 24 March, since which time the drivers report that the engines are working in a satisfactory manner, both steaming better and being lighter on coals.

# Down to Earth Part 3B
## Ex-LBSCR Stock

### Mike King

### Continued from SW53

This concludes our look at ex-LBSCR and Pullman grounded bodies and provides a link to the next instalment in SW55, which will deal with SECR stock.

Between 1905 and 1907, the new LBSCR CME, Douglas Earle Marsh, introduced the high-roofed 'balloon' stock and a relatively small number of coaches (but of many different types) were produced, after which construction then returned to the traditional arc-roofed profile. Many of these coaches were withdrawn in the late 1930s/early 1940s when the need for grounded bodies had increased considerably, so a high proportion of these coaches found a new use 'off wheels'. This is pull-push driving third No. 3836, seen grounded in Lancing Works yard in 1946. This was built as LBSCR No. 1333 in 1906 and was later half of SR pull-push set 741, running until October 1941. It then became departmental coach 1693s and was used for a while at Aldershot before being grounded at Lancing. The driving end is clearly visible, accessed by a sliding door, while the 60-seat passenger saloon was reached via normal hinged doors at each end. SR Diagram 191 was allocated, but there were in fact three different types of 'balloon' auto-trailers amongst the 17 examples of the design. In the background may just be seen an old Pullman car; still on its wheels and one of a pair used for storage and office accommodation – see the final illustration. Lancing Works could boast at least 40 grounded bodies in and around the yard, with a couple more at the station. *D. Cullum*

A 54ft 'balloon' lavatory composite is seen at the entrance to Wimbledon Park electric depot on 22 June 1946 – the station being visible in the background. This began life as LBSCR composite No. 629 in 1905 and was renumbered as SR 6200 after the Grouping, allocated to Diagram 345 – one of just two such vehicles. It is recorded as being formed in SR sets 840 and 927 at various times before withdrawal in December 1940. Grounding followed in 1941. Wimbledon Park depot held at least half a dozen grounded bodies by the late 1940s. *D. Cullum*

This is a 54ft 'balloon' lavatory first; SR No. 7633, seen at Norwood Junction loco shed on 23 July 1946. Built as LBSCR No. 156 in 1907, this ran in SR sets 926 and later 934 – the latter being a first class set for race train traffic – particularly for Ascot and Epsom meetings. It was withdrawn in November 1940 and grounded shortly after. SR Diagram 519 was allocated. Note again that the lower sections of all windows are obscured. Denis Cullum also photographed the coach – just four days later! *R. C. Riley/Transport Treasury*

We now come to luggage vans. This is a 30ft six-wheeler incorporated into a rather larger structure at Godalming Old station (by then a goods depot) and seen in the early 1960s. Another identical van was situated on the far side of the corrugated asbestos-roofed structure seen behind. When examined by the writer in 1969, some scraping of paint at the appropriate eaves panels yielded the SR numbers 2100 and 2113 – although which of the two is seen here cannot now be remembered, but they were both identical. This one was painted green, the other cream. Both were to SR Diagram 975 and both were condemned in February 1940. They were built in 1907/8 as LBSCR numbers 209 and 242 respectively. A similar van, LBSCR No. 270/SR 2178, has been restored to LBSCR umber livery and may be seen on the Bluebell Railway. This is often described as a milk van, but while this may have been one of their cargoes, in reality they could just as easily have carried luggage or parcels, fruit, flowers or any other perishable goods. Most were withdrawn in the 1930s and at least half a dozen were grounded while even more were transferred to departmental use where several, including the one now on the Bluebell Railway, survived to the 1960s. Their railway replacements were, of course, SR utility vans. *Dr. T. Gough*

Quite a large number of 30ft double-ducketed guard's vans were built by the LBSCR, although many were later incorporated into 54ft bogie brake third rebuilds. This left just 23 to become SR Diagram 900 at Grouping and numbered between 739 and 761 in the passenger van stock list. This was SR No. 758 (formerly LBSCR No. 380 of 1897) grounded at Andover Junction shed in March 1935 and photographed soon after grounding. By this time, all four corner lookouts had been removed and replaced by steel sheeting. The van was still there in the 1950s. The 5-compartment composite coach alongside is not of Southern origin – perhaps GWR or even, given the location, ex-Midland & South Western Junction Railway. *A. B. McLeod*

*Above:* **Ex-LBSCR** covered carriage trucks used much the same bodywork as the luggage vans – but in conjunction with end doors and a high-pitched roofline. This is SR Diagram 1164 van 4753 (ex-LBSCR No. 123) grounded at Ashford and seen in 1946, although it had been withdrawn in August 1939 and served as a store at Ashford, still on its wheels, for a number of years thereafter. It was built in 1901. At least four more are recorded as being grounded – the others being located at Lancing Works, Hoo Junction and Selsey (two examples). *D. Cullum*

*Left and below:* Our final pictures of Brighton luggage vans both show SR Diagram 973 milk/fish van No. 2083. In the first shot it is at Callington after World War 2 – still on its wheels but not actually on rails. It was withdrawn in June 1941 and moved to Callington soon after. For just what purpose is not known, but it might have been used as a store for wartime dispersal or possibly for use by the local fruit growers – the area being well known for soft fruit traffic. For this purpose it was painted green, rather than the usual grey – presumably because it was sited within station limits. It remained at the location into the 1950s, when it was returned to the rails and taken to Exmouth Junction carriage & wagon shops. However this was not the end and the van next turned up at Broad Clyst station. It was finally removed from its wheels and grounded in a field near Exeter Airport, where it remains to this day. In the second picture, we see a close-up of one end and, just visible, its former SR number on one side. The other side is now totally devoid of paint. There is just one other coincidence to be noted. This van is number 2083 (in the SR van list) and the Callington picture was taken by Jim Aston. However, the Diagram 64 8-compartment third seen in an earlier picture at Gillingham is also SR number 2083 (but in the carriage stock list) – and was also photographed by Jim Aston! The modern picture is courtesy of Paul Dunn. *J. H. Aston/P. Dunn*

A small number of ex-LBSCR Pullman cars were grounded in the 1930s. This one, at Partridge Green (West Sussex), was formerly *Duchess of Albany* and was one of two grounded at this location (the other was *Princess*). Both were withdrawn in December 1929. *Duchess of Albany* was built in 1890 in the USA and shipped over to Britain for re-assembly and became a parlour car with 32 seats. It was one of four to be tried on the LSWR for a period but by 1912 was running on the LBSCR, where it remained for the rest of its life. Rebuilt at Longhedge Works in 1913, it then became a kitchen car with 22 seats and measured 58ft x 8ft 9in – and weighed 28½ tons – quite a size to be transported away from the railway. The picture dates from April 1950. *D. Cullum*

Two former SER 'Folkestone Club' cars were utilised end-to-end within Lancing Works as offices and storage. They were *Albatross* and *Thistle* and both remained on their wheels but on an isolated portion of track. This is believed to be *Thistle,* but as both cars were identical it might be *Albatross*, seen in September 1949. After serving on the SECR and being put into storage during World War 1, both were purchased by the Pullman Car Company in 1919, along with all the other SECR 'Club' cars, and turned into crimson lake-liveried quasi-Pullmans, where they served until 1938, although neither was actually condemned until January 1940 – presumably their date of 'grounding' at Lancing. Both were built by Metropolitan in 1897 for the South Eastern's Folkestone Club trains, but were later used on boat trains and first class race train services until 1931, when the pair were converted into supply cars for the Pullman Car Company. *F. Foote*

# Spotting on the Somerset & Dorset

## Bill Allen

Bill Allen standing at Evercreech looking up the line from the upper goods yard and facing towards the junction for Highbridge/Bath. He was watching the departure for Bath of No. 75027 with No. 40563 piloting on the 12.21pm all stations Templecombe to Bath. No. 75027 was a new arrival in 1960 at Templecombe MPD and used extensively on local services. Bath had other examples of the class. Built in 1958 she survived withdrawal and is now preserved on the Bluebell Railway, albeit currently on static display at Horsted Keynes. Along with the BR Standard Class 5s which in turn mainly replaced the Bulleid Pacifics on the line, Standard types were the final steam motive power until closure.

In the 1950s and 60s every railway line serving coastal seaside resorts was busy – often to overflowing for the passengers – and stretching railway operating to its limits. One of the most famous of these 'Holiday Routes' was the Somerset and Dorset (S&D). It was no more than a relatively quiet cross-country route on weekdays, with a mix of through passenger trains from Bournemouth to Bath, local services, the 'Branch' to Highbridge and freight. On summer Saturdays the transformation was total, with a succession of 'expresses' from Birmingham, Nottingham, Cleethorpes, Sheffield, Liverpool, Bradford and Manchester conveying expectant holiday makers for their trip to the South Coast.

To add to the operating problems was a series of fearsome grades over the Mendips – culminating at Masbury Summit – and single line sections between Blandford Forum and Templecombe in the South and Midford and Bath at the North end of the line. Foster and Kendall graphically describe the problems in *District Controller's View No 5 S&D 1957*. Suffice to say that men and machines were stretched to breaking point to maintain the service on a Summer Saturday.

As the photographs taken on a trip which my Father, Ron Allen, and I made to Evercreech Junction in the summer of 1960 illustrate, we observed the variety of locomotives, the need for double–heading (with elderly ex-LMS 2P 4-4-0s) and watched the complex timetabling required. We stationed ourselves on the North (Up) side of the line beyond the station platforms on the bank at the end of the up sidings. We could observe that it was no easy start for trains bound for Bath as the gradient was steep (1:105) from the platform. The level goods yard was quite a height above the line – excellent in photographic terms. As an aside the yard contained a dump of metal plates which on closer examination proved to be wagon 'Registered to Carry' plates – most of pre-grouping lines. Permission having been obtained, GCR and Taff Vale Railway examples accompanied us home!

The photographs are sequential – the end of the morning marked the final Bournemouth to the North trains with the southbound peak occurring in early afternoon. The table is an indication from a 1959 timetable of the intensity of the service.

We were privileged to be there and record the trains which incidentally marked a watershed as the Western Region's attempts to reduce double heading meant the arrival in 1960 of 9Fs. This was paralleled by the old order still in evidence with the S&D 7F 2-8-0s and the 2Ps. When we returned in a future year the 2Ps had gone, WR Collett 0-6-0s were in evidence and the era of the holiday makers' regular use of the railway was coming to an end. And this spelt the death knell for the S&D.

(With sincere apologies to Bill for the delay in this appearing.)

No. 40563 stands waiting to pilot a northbound service. Pilots were attached and detached at Evercreech and the siding in between tracks in the platform was often occupied by two, three, or even four locos awaiting such duties. The 2Ps survived one more year in 1961 before finally leaving the line they had served so well. All had been withdrawn by 1962. One of the more bizarre through trains started from Cleethorpes in Lincolnshire and with intermediate calls at Lincoln and Nottingham finally terminated in Exmouth, Devon!

1959 public timetable.

S&D 7F 53804 arrives from Bath on the 6.30am from Birmingham, due at Evercreech at 1.00pm. Built in 1914, one of the original small boilered examples, their primary purpose was to haul heavy freight trains from Bath to Evercreech where the goods trains were marshalled for onward transmission. However, Summer Saturdays saw their employment on passenger services and on this train 53804 has not needed a pilot. All the 7Fs had been withdrawn by 1964 but 53808 and 09 are preserved.

An S&D 7F awaits departure at 1.00pm on the 10.40am Exmouth to Cleethorpes. This train rarely loaded to the point of needing assistance over the Mendips and was a regular diagram for a 7F on Saturdays. In the middle road the 3F waits for a clear platform to then depart at 1.15pm on the 'branch' to Highbridge. Fitting the regular service trains in between the constant flow of through and excursion workings was only possible by careful programming.

Another double-headed southbound express with 9F No. 92204 piloted by a 2P; probably unnecessary as the 9Fs were very capable of hauling trains unassisted. No. 92204 was the locomotive chosen to come to the S&D for trials earlier in the year (29 March 1960). On that day the locomotive, less than a year old having been built in 1959 and in excellent condition, put up an outstanding performance in horrendous rain as Ivo Peters well records. The result of this test was an allocation of four 9Fs for the summer, repeated in the subsequent years before closure of the S&D.

And as a postscript peace descends on the rural scene at Evercreech Junction, central siding prominent with water crane and beyond the footbridge, the level crossing and substantial water tower. The starting signal on the Down road is high above the neat station with waiting room, store rooms, outside Gentleman's Convenience and a two storey Station Master's House. Outside the station had been the Railway Inn, re-named immediately after closure as 'The Silent Whistle'. It survives to this day but now as 'The Natterjack Inn', its railway ancestry seemingly forgotten.

By this period in history the Western Region had allocated No. 3206, a Collett 0-6-0, to Templecombe to replace the former 3F 'Bulldogs' for use on Highbridge branch, local services and also some piloting duties. The 2Ps had also all gone. This S&D 7F had survived and is on the regular turn, Bournemouth to Cleethorpes working. No. 3206 was withdrawn in December 1963. No. 53808 was one of the 1925 batch built by Robert Stephenson with large G9BS boilers. The locomotive received the smaller G9AS in 1953, thereby the five 1925 locomotives became equivalent to the earlier 1914 ones. They remained distinguishable however by being left–hand drive. No. 53808 was withdrawn in March 1964 and consigned to Barry Scrapyard where it languished until rescued and transferred to the West Somerset Railway where preservation and restoration was undertaken. After a second major overhaul the loco is part of the current WSR stock.

# The Railways of the Wandle Valley
# Part 2
## Alan Postlethwaite
(Continued from SW53)

**The Wimbledon – Croydon Line.** The LB&SCR line from Wimbledon to West Croydon opened in 1855. It closed in 1997 for rebuilding as a tramway, reopening in 2000. **Figure 21** shows a London Tram at the new Merton Park halt. This is a little west of the original Merton Park station which was a junction. **Figure 22** shows a 2-WIM unit arriving at the Croydon platform. The next station is Morden Road – see **Figure 23** featuring a Stroudley tank on a push-pull service. Electrification was nigh with the third rail already laid. The station house is of generous size for a single platform station. There was originally a goods siding on the left.

Mitcham station is a contender for the oldest railway station building in the world (**Figure 24**). Built ca. 1803, it was originally a residence. The *News & Mercury* for Mitcham (5.2.72) reported that local historian Tom Francis always described it as a 'guard house' of the Surrey Iron Railway. Either way, it became a station building of the Wimbledon & Croydon Railway which was shortly absorbed into the LB&SCR. It was Grade 2 Listed in 1954 and was later sold off as offices when replaced by a more modest BR booking office.

**Fig 21.** *Alan Postlethwaite*

The Railways of the Wandle Valley

*Above:* **Fig 22.** *John L. Smith © Bluebell Railway Photographic Archive*

*Right:* **Fig 23.** *Merton Memories Collection © London Borough of Merton*
*Below:* **Fig 24.** *Alan Postlethwaite © Bluebell Railway Photographic Archive*

Fig 25. *Colin Hogg © Bluebell Railway Photographic Archive*

At Mitcham Junction, **Figure 25** shows a Sunday excursion from Peterborough to Hove via Steyning. Coming off the super-elevated Streatham curve, the train is double headed by class U1 Mogul No. 31904 and Light Pacific No. 34047 *Callington*. Such trains usually exchanged locomotives from BR(E) alongside Blackfriars goods station.

Mitcham Junction was a double junction to accommodate services between Streatham and Sutton. It once had a bay and a coal siding. **Figure 26** shows the Croydon end in 1962 while **Figure 27** shows the parallel tramway in 2019. This is where the Hackbridge branch of the Surrey Iron Railway curved away to the right.

Hackbridge station has a new yellow brick booking office with the original LB&SCR station building beyond, now put to other uses (**Figure 28**). Carshalton station (**Figure 29**) was rebuilt in 1902, as recorded on a plaque above the entrance. Its country mansion style was unique on the LB&SCR.

*Left:* **Fig 26.** *Alan Postlethwaite © Bluebell Railway Photographic Archive*
*Below:* **Fig 27.** *Alan Postlethwaite*

The Railways of the Wandle Valley

**Fig 28.** *Alan Postlethwaite*
**Fig 29.** *Alan Postlethwaite*

**Fig 30.** *John L. Smith © Bluebell Railway Photographic Archive*
**Fig 31.** *John L. Smith © Bluebell Railway Photographic Archive*

Fig 32. *Alan Postlethwaite*

The Southern's Beddington Lane halt had a single platform in a rural setting (**Figure 30**). By contrast, the setting of Waddon Marsh halt was totally industrial (**Figure 31**). The humble wooden island platform was surrounded by a gas works, two power stations, a sewage farm, hospital and factories.

Waddon station, on the Croydon-Sutton line, is in the Southern's art deco style but in brick (**Figure 32**). The railway from Wimbledon rejoined the system at West Croydon. **Figure 33** shows class C2X No. 32546 approaching West Croydon with an Up freight. Much coal traffic used to trundle through here from Deptford Wharf or the Kent coalfield en route to the gas works and power stations at Waddon.

**Figure 34** shows the art deco frontage of West Croydon station. It originally had SR 'sunshine' lettering, enticing one to take a ride. The station also has a side entrance in Station Road, seen on the right in **Figure 35**. This is overlooked by an eclectic mix of Victorian and contemporary town buildings and the bus station The London Trams pass on a one-way circular route to New Addington, Elmers End (SER) and Beckenham Junction (LC&DR). All four principal constituents of the Southern Railway are therefore connected by the bright new trams. Long gone are the Surrey Iron chaldrons of dung, fullers earth, manure and other delicacies of the early 19th century. After 215 years of evolution, public transport in Outer South Suburbia continues to impress and amaze.

Fig 33. *John L. Smith © Bluebell Railway Photographic Archive*

**Fig 34.** *Alan Postlethwaite*
**Fig 35.** *Alan Postlethwaite*

## Further Reading

1. *The Wandle Trail*, Merton Borough website.
2. Mcgow, Peter, *Notes on the Surrey Iron Railway*, 2001, The Wandle Industrial Museum website.
3. Disused Stations website.
4. Wikipedia for notes on the stations.
5. Edith's Streets – London Local History website.
6. *Northern Line Disused Features*, Raggajohn website.

# John Gaywood Click
## 'Engineering the Southern' Part 5

## Working with Bulleid in Ireland

Some readers may wonder why a topic related to Ireland should appear in 'SW'. To answer this I should first speak in general terms and they are: if an explanation is required, then perhaps more thought should be given to the title!

Simply put however, Mr Bulleid ranks high in personalities relevant to the Southern Railway, he has his followers and his detractors whilst his steam engines, rolling stock and electric units lasted well into British Railways days and are no doubt remembered by many.

None of the four pre-nationalisation Chief Mechanical Engineers remained in post long into the corporate BR era but as stated, many of their creations did, and consequently whilst we stood (or sat) and admired 'Merchant Navy', 'West Country', 'Battle of Britain', 'Q1', '4-SUB' and 'Waterloo and City' stock I wonder how many considered what he might have been up to

**The bus engine mounted at the rear of the tender on No. 356.**
*A. R. Pocklington*

after he had left the Southern. John Click tells us exactly that. The latter's work with Bulleid at the CIE workshops at Inchicore just outside Dublin witnessed yet another Bulleid dream emerge into reality. This was the Turf Burner, or perhaps, as it may be described, 'Leader Mk 2'.

Readers may also have noticed that whilst we have hinted at John Click's involvement with No. 36001, any detailed comments he may have made have not appeared in this series. I have to say this is deliberate on the part of this editor, as these have been deliberately held back to be included instead in the revised book on Leader due to be released in June 2021.

In the same book we will be including a brief appendix on Turf Burner and for the same reason as mentioned above. Consequently, in order to round off this series on John Click we have pleasure in including a limited version of the same appendix here.

As is stated above, the Turf Burner might equally be called 'Leader Mk 2'. Much of how it evolved and why has been well covered by Ernie Shepherd in his 2004 book* and need not be repeated here. Suffice to say that after a failed attempt at purchasing No. 36001 and her sisters from BR, Bulleid had this one remaining opportunity to prove a modern steam engine could be a viable proposition. Hence 'Leader Mk 2' is most certainly the appropriate label to use as the two shared so much in common. That similarity extended to the double-bogie, all adhesion locomotive, again with chain drive but also with one important difference to 'Leader Mk 1'. In 'Leader Mk 2', the actual 'engine' unit within the bogie was easily interchangeable. Here was one of the features Bulleid himself stated he should have incorporated into the original Leader design, and no doubt he would, had time allowed the original engine to have been developed further. Visually too, the two were 'similar', but take care: we use the word 'similar' with caution as even a quick glance will show that the Turf Burner had a more centrally placed cab – central that is along the length of the engine, the boiler/firebox also not offset to one side – hence both crew were together. The fact the engine was also intended to burn peat meant that with a low calorific value fuel, large quantities had to be carried and so at each end there were large hoppers for fuel.

It cannot be denied that the Bulleid Turf Burner worked and worked well. A few changes might have been desirable, even necessary but it remained a *working* engine. Another similarity to Leader was it was also just a single prototype (this is the literal truth, as 'Leader' Nos. 36002-5 were never totally complete and certainly never tested/operated) although Bulleid must have realised that by the time Turf Burner was eventually complete and running, steam, fuelled by whatever means, was in terminal decline in Ireland.

As we have said, Turf Burner worked – on turf that is – and like Leader (which of course burnt coal) it never was modified/converted to burn oil. But just like Leader, history would repeat itself. It was in the wrong place, and at the wrong time. A decade earlier and it could have been a different story. Click, who was with Bulleid in Ireland for some time, confirms this thought, 'Far too long had been taken in Ireland too, chasing countless elusive ideas. In all honesty, and modesty too, I had said to OVB, "Look we cannot do everything on this one either," or his 'Turf Burner' would never have turned a wheel.'

Click writes, 'Bulleid didn't always realise how much more limited in scale were the facilities at his disposal in Eire, and expected near miracles over his favourite projects; but also often got them. Quite what, or who, started him off on the idea of burning turf in a steam locomotive isn't clear, but the fact that it had never been done really satisfactorily would have been enough, for it offered him a challenge of the kind he most liked. It was also very politically acceptable in some quarters: especially as peat-burning power stations had been commissioned some time earlier.'

It is perfectly reasonable to believe Bulleid's appointment in Ireland was based on a requirement to develop an efficient turf-burning locomotive. Even so we may ask the question (privately perhaps), did Bulleid agree to such a proposal or was it instead more of a transparent promise with Bulleid instead really wishing to continue his development of his 'ultimate' steam design? Even if the latter, it is interesting to note that he still did not copy the ideals of M. Chapelon. We might similarly ask 'who approached whom'? Did Bulleid approach CIE or might CIE have even approached Bulleid? We cannot be certain although the former would perhaps seem the most likely especially with Bulleid's persuasive charm.

Whatever the case, Owen Wynne, a senior member of staff at the time Bulleid was in Ireland, recalled how, once settled in his office at Inchicore, he had requested we set up an experiment to burn turf in the Babcock and Wilcox stationary boilers in the power house. 'I arranged to have a very large quantity of turf stacked in front of the firebox and six labourers were engaged to continuously throw peat into the firebox to maintain pressure. In due course OVS (*sic*) was telephoned to the effect that the boiler …. was maintaining the required pressure.' On arrival 'when the safety valve blew' OVS was overheard by the labourers to say, 'Well, it burns,' a story that 'was to go the rounds for a long time afterwards' said Owen. 'Why was he so surprised, everyone in Ireland knew that turf was the primary fuel source in Ireland down the centuries.'

How John Click came to Inchicore to work with Bulleid appears to stem from August 1954 when he travelled to Ireland on holiday, but perhaps with the double intention of what we might nowadays be referred to as a (personal) 'fact finding mission', allied to rumours that no doubt would have been circulating in engineering circles at both Rugby – where Click was then working – as well as elsewhere.

Again John Click's notes are not in any order and again there are several drafts of the same piece and similarly there are chunks missing. Even so it is possible to glean that for his vacation he based himself at Dublin and consequently was close to the main works at Inchicore. As he also admits, '….what Mr Bulleid was up to was one magnet.'

This was clearly not a spontaneous visit either, for prior to travel Click had written to Mr Meredith, the CME of the GNR(I). (Richard W. Meredith came to the GNR(I) from the GSWR having been working with Maunsell at Inchicore. He was appointed GNR(I) works manager at the start of 1926. He was especially interested in diesel engines, developing railbuses and railcars, patenting the Howden-Meredith steel and pneumatic railbus tyre. He became CME of the GNR(I) on 1 January 1951 and retired in the Spring of 1957.) Meredith generously responded with footplate passes for the GNR(I). Click also wrote in advance to CIE who were similarly gracious including the opportunity for a works visit and a similar footplate trip. In consequence of what happened later it is very possible Bulleid may even have been the one to 'pull the necessary strings' probably remembering the name of his former pupil.

Click again takes up the story, 'At midday (during his August 1954 sojourn) I was back in the Inchicore Offices and, nothing ventured nothing gained, asked if it was possible to see the CME. "Ah no, he's abroad; but would you like to see the Chief Draughtsman for a minute?' (A few years earlier Bulleid had been commuting between Brighton and Inchicore both to oversee 'Leader' at the former location and at the commencement of his work with CIE. By 1954 of course, visits away from Ireland would not have been connected with British Railways. Interesting too is Bulleid's comment when he finally left BR, as he thanked the Railway Executive for letting him get so much useful data 'for future work' – and now of course we know what that was intended to be!)

Back at Inchicore and JGC comments (the verbal descriptions of the wonderful Irish dialect are those written by Click), 'Paddy Mulvany was genial, but couldn't tell me, "… anyt'ing about the Turf Burner, f'r it's a national secret, y'understand." I did; but then played my trump card. I had taken with me a copy of a 7mm drawing of the Leader, and produced it now. "T'at's a fine drawing," said he, "did you do it…. you did, can I have it?" After studying it, he beckoned outside, "Woodjou bring me t'at diagram of the turf borner for a minute!" He kept it upside down tantalisingly, but that was no real problem for we at Rugby had got used to reading that way up. It was one of the only two methods there of finding anything out! I thanked Mr. Mulvany, went into town and spent the next two hours sketching all that I'd seen – both ways up.'

A few days later Click wrote a 'thank you' letter – to Mulvany perhaps? – but concluding with '… if there is ever an opportunity of doing original work under you I would seriously consider dragging my English anchors.' 'I hadn't the slightest idea that might either be possible, or practicable. The letter went off and I gave it no more thought, but on the Friday I was putting on my overalls before footplating home from Rugby to Euston on the 4.57pm Up, ex-Llandudno, when I was unexpectedly wanted on the phone. "Is thut you, John?" came a familiar voice, "If you want thut job in Dublin, yer to apply for it!" OVB must have rung C.S. Cocks in Derby at once. I had that rare feeling of being needed: walking on air, but what to do?'

In John Click's draft, what follows next is a slightly strange recollection which is also certainly out of date. 'At Inchicore I was given a guide and I asked him to show me the Turf Burner. "Ah no," he said, "I mustn't show you t'at," but adding that he truly didn't know where it was. Eventually right at the far end of the works I thought I'd found it – there was an expanse of dirty grey dimly seen through two lines of carriage windows…. Yes! "Now," I said hopefully, "If you stay here and I walk round the end of that coach you won't have shown me it will you?" "Oh, I will not," he agreed. As luck had it there was a coach alongside from which a good general view looked possible; so hoisting myself up over its buffers and in through the open corridor end I crept on all fours towards my chosen, and fortunately open, corridor window. As I slowly rose I knew I was being watched, in that very compartment were four men frozen as if in a waxworks – playing cards! After a few seconds we all burst out laughing with relief: 'deuce' certainly, or at least a draw.' We know Click was present at Inchicore during the tests with burning peat and then later on with the Turf Burner engine. We believe he also returned to the UK in 1958 so this is likely to have been a subsequent visit, possibly even when the engine had been set aside.

With more certainty, and returning to 1954, Click did indeed take up the job in Ireland. 'Next summer (1955), I persuaded Ronald (Ron) Pocklington (who had come to us at Rugby direct from Vulcan Foundry) to come to Dublin with me. He was very interested in everything Bulleid was doing and had by then got to know No. 35022 at the Test Plant and had also ridden to Dover and back with me on No. 35028 working the 'Golden Arrow'. His was a more academic approach to a problem; whereas mine was more practical, so we tended to complement each other. On *Clan Line* RP took it all in good part until we crashed across the diamonds and plunged, rolling, through Sevenoaks, past the last electrified sidings and into the long tunnel. Diving in at 65 we accelerated steadily in total darkness until very near the end a spot of light. Initially, purple, then brown – getting larger – yellow and suddenly out into brilliant daylight – racing downhill at 85mph! It was a good baptism. Nothing subsequent did anything to diminish his admiration for the locomotive or its designer.' What Click and Pocklington's official job titles were is not reported, suffice to say they were both 'Assistants' to Bulleid (assuming this to be correct, it is something of a coincidence that this was exactly the same term as had been applied between Bulleid and Gresley). The two, Click and Pocklington, were also clearly not, as has been reported previously, 'seconded from BR' which in itself could have led to all sorts of suggestions relative to Bulleid's then current work.

Click himself speaks of his own first experiences in fond terms, 'Ireland as a whole was a wonderful retreat for the lover of the old and the quaint, but it was no way to run the various railways. Many locomotive engineers who later became more famous on this side of the water started in Ireland. Too many of their engines were still there in the fifties, though disappearing fast. Bulleid's father-in-law's (H. A. Ivatt's) dinky little 2-4-2 tank actually hauled his Turf Burner out of the erecting shop. She regularly worked 'The Cab' (we later learned this to have been the nickname of a 6-wheel coach) down to Kingsbridge station taking Inchicore staff to lunch there – that is until a shunter let two coaches down on to the six-wheeler, drove it up on to her buffer beam and wrote it off.' Without further reference (and in a caption for a photograph he clearly intended to use in his own book – the photograph has not been located) he speaks of other engines he observed from the period as well. 'This Aspinall 4-4-0 was standing in for No. 42 which must have been having a washout that day. The 'Cab' is about to leave tender first and will return after lunch with the engine propelling the six-wheeler ahead of her. A number of these charming museum pieces were still doing quite important work when I left in 1958 and all had been superheated many years before, but I never saw Bulleid register the slightest interest in any of them……….then there was this small Midland 2-4-0 designed by Atock which had worked the Boat Train from Westland Row in 1956. The volute springs on the leading axle are very unusual…… more recently, and still very competent, were some of the Maunsell 'moguls' adapted to the 5' 3" gauge from sets of parts bought very cheaply from Woolwich after WW1………Watson, who produced some four-cylinder 4-6-0s based on Churchward's design, seems to have made one or two cardinal errors.

No. 356 in its converted state to burn turf and seen at Inchicore in 1954. The engine is depicted with the original Crosti type pre-heaters either side of the boiler. These were much altered later. *A. R. Pocklington*

He either believed all Swindon geese were swans or couldn't cope very well, or both, come to that! All had been drastically rebuilt as two-cylinder engines, nearly all different; and two, though I missed seeing them at work, had Caprotti valve gear which Matt Devereux said had made them into very good engines indeed......
........I was up there looking for parts to cannibalise for the Turf Burner: such as ejectors and snifting valves – and I did find what I wanted!'

We have jumped forward slightly as some years before this and to test the idea of burning peat (dried peat had been used for centuries as a domestic fuel in Scandinavia, Scotland and of course Ireland) Bulleid had a stationary test rig erected within Inchicore Works. This included an electric motor driving a large fan arranged to force draught to a spare boiler from a 101 class locomotive which was mechanically stoked from an outsize bunker behind the rig. To simulate the intended subsequent Crosti-type feed-heater, a second, smaller boiler was installed facing the other way with both sharing a common smokebox. The combined chimney emerged from the firehole on this front boiler. The boiler was manually fed with sods of peat, '....by about six firemen.....and the safety valve kept lifting.' (Perhaps even the same labourers from the earlier power station experiment!) Upon seeing it Click commented, 'It was difficult: no, let's face it, impossible not to laugh, but there it was! Think, though. This rig was a 'lash- up', but designed by a bold man, unafraid of ridicule and ready to do new research work into a problem.'

Possibly even preceding this workshop test rig, the Chief Chemist had conducted his own experiments by stuffing smouldering turf up an old boiler tube and then blowing it with compressed air. He had got, transitorily, very high temperatures. Even so the risk was that at such high temperatures peat ash could form clinker and which explains the same question raised by Bulleid later. One thing Click does add, is that even at the time of his visit(s) and subsequent employment, there was a distinct paucity of records as to what tests had been undertaken (presumably with peat?) and the results thereof.

Having satisfied himself the principles were sound, Bulleid, as on the Southern, looked around for a guinea-pig engine on which to try out his ideas. Chosen was a former Great Southern & Western Railway K3 class 2-6-0 No. 356 as the test bed. The modifications made included a new firebox fitted with tuyeres (these are orifices through which air is blown into the firebox to aid combustion), two Crosti pre-heaters either side of the boiler, which took heat from the exhaust to pre-heat the feed water, plus further pre-heating coils in the tender water tank. With the exhaust thus routed back along the engine and through the tender water it is not surprising to report the actual chimney was on the rear of the tender. Turf was fed into the firebox by means of an Archimedean screw; although short of switching the screw off, the amount fed was difficult if not impossible to regulate. A Leyland internal combustion engine (from a bus) was also mounted on a small four-wheel wagon 'permanently' attached to the rear of the tender; this was used to drive the fan that created draft for the tuyeres as the firebox was otherwise sealed. (Recall also the comment from Paddy Mulvany at the time of his Brighton visit referring to the chimney on the rear of the tender, 'By George, t'ats the very forst t'ing he wanted when he got here as well' – which of course referred to No. 356.)

We have no definite date, but we do know from correspondence that No. 356 was working by some time late in 1951 and made at least one trip to Cork, as engine-tender-four-wheel-wagon. As so modified (the bus-engine was a slightly later addition as is mentioned below) it meant that a Cork trip was possible. Unfortunately the ensemble was too long to fit on the Cork turntable and with the thought of returning tender first over that distance – 163 miles from Inchicore (or should that even be 'bus engine' first?) totally out of the question, so it was necessary to separate the vehicle on which the bus engine was mounted, with each turned separately and then reattached.

Click adds his own comments about his first experience of No. 356 probably during his 1954 visit and before he took up his formal appointment in Dublin, for he adds Bulleid 'cannily'

Lowering one of the two-cylinder (conventional Walschaerts valve gear) engines into a power bogie, June 1957. It could be achieved – the removable engine unit – and given time might well have been incorporated into Leader.

said, 'Well Click, if you can wait until tomorrow you can go out on the experimental locomotive,' I instantly decided 'Yes, please.' Finding a way of 'explaining' why I'd not be back at Rugby next morning was a formality…..'

'I was taken up to No. 356 which from the look of it hadn't turned a wheel for many months. The foreman had been told to prepare it for its run next day. "Sh'yer can't go out on t'at t' ing; – it's a heap of scrap," he said – altogether accurately! I had a good look round it, and had my doubts whether they'd ever get steam in it again. All the plates of the left-hand truck spring were broken (this was the truck carrying the bus engine) and I remember thinking if there's going to be a derailment it will only be at low speed in the yard. If we made it to the main line it would run.

'Working pressure was reached before I joined the locomotive. No. 356 had been spruced up a bit, and sported what in the UK would be express headlamps and had a willing crew aboard expectantly wondering, as I was, what would happen next. I climbed up, got a welcome, had a look at the fire first, watched as the stoker was operated and got an impression of how turf behaved.

'Draught, provided by the bus engine driven induction fan on the wagon behind the huge tender, was 'controlled' by a wire that disappeared over a pulley on the tender front and somehow reached its accelerator. This additional bus engine had become necessary as on the first trials, possible when the engine had failed to achieve a successful round trip between Dublin and Cork (evidently the 'standard' test for a new engine), it was evident that forced draught was not on; and the original little steam turbines, notoriously uneconomical at part load, also gobbled up precious steam. The bus-driven fan meant that forced (blown) draught gave way to induced, or sucking draught. Leaks henceforward would be into rather than out of the system. Space constraints though meant there was nothing for it but to mount the new arrangements on the separate wagon hitched behind the tender – even so, something else for the critics to jibe about.

'The firing was very much an all or nothing affair. When the fireman wanted more steam he turned on the 'worum' (the stoker screw) and pulled the chain (which really was from some unfortunate loo) whereupon the bus engine went ' vrooOOM' taking a lot of the fire through the tubes, the smokebox, the bank of feed heaters, the labyrinth of ducts over the cab and through the tender, out of its back, into more flexible joints, through the fan and out of its 'chimney' in a gigantic plume of what would have been called 'Golden rain'; but all before there was time to say "turf smoke."

'It wanted gentle handling so I asked if I could have a go. Soon with the bus engine ticking over quite slowly and the stoker delivering a steady amount of turf she began to make steam quickly, and blew off keeping the safety valve up against the injector for a while. We were still by the Erecting Shop but it looked quite promising. We rumbled off with the exhaust beat getting lost somewhere in the tender but it didn't matter anyway

– because steam production was by fan – totally divorced from the way the locomotive was worked. It was, not very surprisingly, possible to lose the fire in a trice or to smother it with too much new turf: after all we were dealing with a fuel with less than half the calorific value of an average coal and a quarter by weight of what went in was water, tending to put the fire out. Imagine it: for every ten pounds of 'air-dried' turf that went on there were also two pints of water! Fly ash was a problem: it floated away prettily, and possibly harmlessly, still ignited. The danger was the larger, smouldering lumps, and what about clinker?'

'On the way up the bank to Clondalkin I began to get the hang of it – watching the fire and with the exhaust colour just the same as at Rugby – though everything happened faster. The quality of the firebed changed very quickly, it was a full-time and very demanding job. The speed was only low but we held the water level quite easily. When we arrived everyone was pleased: "Ah, you had hor steaming grand" said one, "we could've gone to Cork, sure we could." It would certainly have been nice to have gone on a bit further; I was just getting the feel of it.

'We dropped back down to Inchicore in the dark and what a sight it must have made from the lineside; fan wagon and tender first! Enough to make any Ballyfermot man who was 'after having taken a few' sign the pledge.

'Just a touch of bus engine and a little turf every minute or so and we were enveloped in the beautiful scent of properly burned turf; delicate turf sparks floating by and me feeling here's a job I could tackle and get my teeth into. No. 356 never did venture out on to the main line again, it didn't need to, testing could and should be done standing still.

'Back in OVB's office he wanted to know what I thought. I said that seeing the problem had made me far more certain that it could be solved, but that a much larger grate area would be needed.'

But what 'problem' was it that Click was referring to? There is nothing in Click's notes. A reasonable assumption was that Bulleid had asked for Click's view as to whether peat was a suitable fuel, or something similar. To be fair Bulleid probably knew the answer himself but may well have been 'testing out the man' or even seeking confirmation of his own beliefs.

'Whatever, Bulleid continued, "Was there any clinker problem?" he asked. My emphatic "No, none at all" was said in a way that must have given him thought, as he added, seemingly thinking out loud, "...so no sulphur either..." I made the point about there being no need to risk main line failure and he agreed, but said that 'politically' it had to be seen to run. I remembered No. 32039's misfortune at Earlswood and fully understood.'

'At that time No. 356 had Crosti type pre-heaters on both sides and draught was already supplied by the bus engine driven fan on a wagon behind. It had previously made one fateful trip to Cork but failed on the way back, I was later told, and then seemed to have been dumped. OVB had copied the best (of what was new), or so it seemed but, in any case, Crosti had not put in for an Irish Patent. He actually turned up at Inchicore on one occasion, Matt Devereux told me later, and was seen by Johnny Johnston but got no joy. Quite what made Bulleid change the heaters is not clear, although possibly it was suggested by Ricardo at Shoreham (Bulleid had obviously maintained this relationship after he had left England). By next summer (when I went over again) large

**No. 2 engine running in No. 1 bogie, and on just 5psi of steam from an outside source.** *A. R. Pocklington*

John Gaywood Click 'Engineering the Southern' Part 5

As with Leader the final drive was by chain with an unsymmetrical drive; but no problems with broken crank-axles this time. Unlike on Leader the springs were not flood lubricated. *A. R. Pocklington*

The centrally placed (along the longitudinal axis) boiler/firebox. The whole was of square construction with the shape a source of some concern to some in case scale might accumulate in the corners and lead to wasting. *A. R. Pocklington*

panniers containing banks of finned aluminium heaters had been substituted. These were developed, it transpired later, from miniature cast aluminium alloy boilers designed by Ricardo for supplying small steam engines for use in what we would now call 'developing countries'.'

Click continues on the subject of No. 356. 'A bus engine was all very well on the guinea-pig but the 'prototype' had to have turbines and when I arrived at Dublin early in 1956 they had not only been ordered but soon arrived.' Referring now to both himself and Pocklington, '…..nothing was more important for us than to get some actual experience of 'the turf' for ourselves; so accordingly No. 356 got altered yet again. For a week, and until the turf feed screw broke up, we did a series of useful tests which gave us the only data we had on what went on. The only thing we couldn't do was to use the superheater. What steam we did make and that wasn't used by the auxiliaries, went out of the safety valves: it represented all that was left for traction and didn't look much. Even so, testing was very labour-intensive, but invaluable.'

Meanwhile what would later be designated 'CC1' was slowly taking shape in the workshops at Inchicore. Click had arrived after the principal design had been agreed, which like Leader consisted of a double bogie (six wheels/three axles per bogie) steam engine having a central boiler with a cab on either end of the boiler after which came a large turf hopper. The idea being that the crew would be able to have a reasonable view of the track ahead by looking either side of the turf bunker. The cabs were not connected but the driver and fireman would always be together. In order to maximise the heating surface the boiler and firebox was also almost rectangular even if this was a constant source of concern to some of the VIP visitors who later saw and indeed travelled on the engine. (Appertaining to this

**Archimedean screws either end (Berkeley-type mechanical stoker) to feed turf into the firebox from either bunker.** A. R. Pocklington

topic, Click comments, 'The boiler for the Turf Burner, by its extraordinary design, frightened everybody; it was only a question of degree. (Everyone, that is, except OVB himself!) When Cocks came over and rode with us he told me, "They've all been invited, but they're afraid of the boiler so they've sent me!" When I first saw the boiler it had previously been fired, we were told, by, "sods of turf using pitchforks" with ring blowers in the chimneys at each end producing draught. The water level was said to have fluctuated wildly whenever its safety valve blew, a fact we verified two years later and cured by adding to the number of U-tubes connecting the central firebox to the two cuboid 'barrels'. Subsequent theoretical calculations by Ron Pocklington estimated a steaming rate of 20,000 lb/hr.'

Click's own notes now add a totally new twist to the design which shows that yet again Bulleid was not content with the design as it stood, for he comments, 'Shortly afterwards Paddy Mulvany disclosed that "Mr Bulleid is not after making up his mind about superheating"; and, later again, OVB himself told me he was looking for "plenty of wet steam so I can use the Anderson/Holcroft compression condensing system." Even if that system had ever worked as claimed (and remember it had been tried on 'N' class 2-6-0 No. A816 in the 1930s) there was a serious fallacy in his argument, simply because the amount of heat in the exhaust (with saturated steam) would be more in total due to the far higher steam consumption. In other words the classic reasons for superheating remained unchanged. By then, that meant radiant heating coils in the firebox which seemed 'out' (because of the desire to put an oil fire in later on) or to do the best we could with a 'superheater' (even if it might not be much better than a 'steam dryer') in the smokebox. That we did, but not before being sent over to London to hear what Holcroft had to say. I'm afraid we found him very unconvincing.'

This is one of the few times oil is mentioned as fuel for CC1 but it is not clear if this meant heavy bunker type fuel or conventional diesel – probably the former. Just to show CC1 was also only a stage along the road of development, the cylinder design that was actually installed was not, according to Click, what Bulleid had originally envisaged. Instead, '……he hankered for a three cylinder one (still) with sleeve valves and we would have 'had a go' if time had been open-ended. It is also just possible that the loco might have had five cylinders!' Click does not elaborate further on this almost mind-numbing suggestion and we are left to speculate on what if anything Bulleid had in fact learnt from his experience with Nos. 2039 and 36001? Without wishing to be personally rude, it appears to have been 'not a lot'. (The present writer when *attempting* to discuss both Leader and Turf Burner with John Click many years ago showed Mr Click a sketch – since lost – of a double-acting cylinder having a central con-rod driving two horizontally opposed pistons, in appearance similar to that of a Westinghouse air pump. The question asked was, '…did this relate to the Turf Burner or Leader?' by inference the answer was the Turf Burner, with the additional rider, '…we discounted that as unworkable very early on.' Sadly too, this was one of the very few occasions John Click was willing to provide a practical comment.)

John Gaywood Click 'Engineering the Southern' Part 5

**Nearing completion at Inchicore in May 1957.** *A. R. Pocklington*

Within the Inchicore workshops history would again repeat as had occurred at Brighton with No. 36001, as a finished bogie complete with its installed steam engine, was run in in the Erecting Shop with steam supplied from an Aspinall 4-4-0 outside. It only needed about 5psi to be kept happily ticking over. Corrugated steam pipes of the Alton type were fitted which flexed to allow for bogie movement. This was a repeat of their successful use on No. 36001. The exhaust from both bogies was also combined. The actual engine complete with cylinders was removable, the idea being to substitute a fresh engine at an intermediate repair. The cost of a small number of spares would have been economically justified had a fleet of fifty been built as was indeed the original intention. As to how and when this figure was arrived at, and equally when it was cancelled, is not reported.

Click again: 'Because the Turf Burner was fan-draughted, the exhaust steam did nothing – a fact that OVB continually complained about; he wanted its heat used, and he was quite right. His favourite ideas were using the Holcroft/Anderson (Click refers to it as Anderson/Holcroft) compression condensing system and/or for drying the peat itself. Unfortunately all the available time (and space) were taken up making the loco go. Other worthy aims had to take second place, but we compromised by making it possible to turn some exhaust back into the tanks until the water got too hot for the Worthington feed pumps to deal with.'

All of the earlier trials had been leading up to the building of the main locomotive, later numbered 'CC1' – once again Bulleid's numbering scheme was to the fore. No name was ever carried.

When CC1 was finally completed in 1957 – the same year its predecessor No. 356 would be scrapped – Click had the rare privilege of being the first to move the engine in steam. Decades later we can only imagine the pride he must have felt, as in his own words, 'At last the day came to move the Turf Burner for the first time. To a bystander there I am sure my efforts would have looked very much as Granshaw's had to me on No. 36001 at Brighton. Bulleid had arrived much too early, waited a while and then told me to be sure and phone for him before I moved. I hadn't phoned but he drove up again later and then must have stayed. I cannot think now, as the only person there who had seen what had been done (and not done) at Brighton, why I didn't get a 'buddy' loco over to act as a helper, or at least to be an anchor. She wouldn't go either way for some time. One wheel was in a very low rail joint but she wasn't in full gear either, due to a part of the steam reverser having been removed and put back upside-down. Once this was put right she did move.......I had rehearsed this moment for months; in most of my dreams it had been easier!' (Again the similarities to No. 36001's first moves are uncanny.)

As with Leader, and before that No. 2039, trial runs with empty stock were run from stations to replicate normal working/timings. It is believed this is at one of the Dublin stations. *A. R. Pocklington*

After this Click talks of a variety of experiences running with the engine on the main line, such as, 'To make sure what was going on underneath I had a seat welded on to the bogie and rode eleven miles on it. I told the driver it was deuced uncomfortable and I didn't want to be down there long. Michael Keely took me at my word and reached a steady 60mph. It was enthralling to see the miniature valve gear (NOT this time in an oil bath) though the crankshaft was whizzing round at some nine revs a second and to feel the fan effect of the wheels. Back at Inchicore I had the seat burnt off, but OVB was very disappointed – he wanted a go too, and I believe he would have.'

'Another occasion was when R. C. Bond and Bulleid's brother-in-law H. G. (George) Ivatt came over and rode on the turf burner; we got delayed at Clondalkin. Mr Bulleid travelled with us a number of times, once got up in a very French beret and wearing a white coat with gloves. (On another occasion M. Louis Armand, General Manager of the French railway system, was also an interested observer. M. Armand had been inventor of the TIA *'Traitement Integral Armand'* water treatment system.) I tried several times to get him to drive but without success. But he chatted all the while; about the smooth ride, the hotness of the peat fire, and "Look at the interest those cattle are taking in us – they always recognised anything new!"'

**There was similarity with Leader in so far as the engine was carried on two six-wheel bogies. Above the frames however much was different not least the driver and fireman being together in one of the two cabs – but again each was only accessible from one side. The matter of crew safety in the event of an accident and the engine turning over appears not to have been mentioned in Ireland. The location of what was another test run is not given.** *A. R. Pocklington*

Click also mentions another footplate observer, Cyril Fry, famed for his 'O' gauge Irish International Railway and Tramway System. Fry knew CIE's Chairman well and, through him, eventually got drawings out of OVB and had a model running – he even contrived to get an authentic turf smell from it. He added, 'Cyril and I both lived in Churchtown and I had the pleasure of seeing his railway several times; but, though I tried hard to get OVB to pay a visit he always said, "Oh no, if I went up I'd have the whole works making models, and that wouldn't do at all."'

By 1958 it must have been obvious there was to be no duplication of the design, but this did not stop interest from overseas. Such as when in that year there was a visitation from the Birmingham Railway Carriage and Wagon Co. They had been invited over to look at the way the drive from the engine was coupled to the three axles by chains – superb even torque of course – but again this was as per its predecessor No. 36001. (No failed crank axles on CC1 either.) In the same year CC1 was painted green and had a second set of smoke deflectors added '.....eau-de-nil' sash and a yellow warning pattern to OVB's own sketch......,' according to Click.

Click had also returned to full time work with British Railways at Rugby by now, but was a visitor again later and shortly after the Institution of Locomotive Engineers' Summer Meeting in Dublin for which OVB had tried without success to get him back. Click adds – again we may imagine perhaps wistfully, 'The 'urgency of work' at the Testing Station had ruled that out.' It seems also that on the morning the Institution Members were to pay their visit, OVB had only managed to get No. CC1 into steam at the last minute – nobody had lit her up. So, later on he got her round to the head of the exhibits where, being last, she thus became first! This was an advantage because no shunting had to be done to get her out; hence after OVB had taken E. S. Cox to Clondalkin (4½ miles from Dublin) and back everybody wanted to do the same, and many did: '...they are all steam men at heart' OVB wrote. All marvelled, although whether that was wholly true or not, at Bulleid's persistence in getting authority for an even more innovative design than the 'Leader' to present to them for their delight. CC1 stole the show; but what followed? For John Click it was one last drive to Sallins, 17¾ miles, then 'finis': 'I had made the first move and also the last. She was quietly cut up in 1965.' Perhaps the VIP visitors were not really marvelling at the engineering prowess of the design but were instead seeing what might almost be regarded as a fairground attraction.

That Summer 1958 ILE visit was also the swansong for CC1. All day long it had moved up and down, up and down to Clondalkin giving footplate rides to VIPs. It had proved that peat could after all be used as a locomotive fuel. The order for fifty examples, for which a million punts had been kept in CIE's budget for some years, was gently forgotten.

What we should also remember is that CC1 just like No. 36001 never entered revenue-earning service. But unlike the Leader it never had to be hauled home, not even after a minor collision (Click does not afford any details of this) and this despite the jaunty angle of the buffers. It also never caused a minute's delay to other traffic and established a good reputation for speed out on the Dublin-Cork main line AND it could even be said to have earned a small amount of revenue for the CIE; as on the occasion when it ventured to Kildare on a test run (30 miles) – one of the regular trial destinations. On this particular day the station master came and asked whether, 'as a great favour,' the engine could move some wagons through the station for him; CC1 obliged. This was one of the few 'revenue earning' tasks the locomotive ever did although folklore has it the engine was also used to make a few trips from Inchicore to North Wall on transfer freights.

To conclude, as we know John Click returned to British Railways and his work at Rugby. He subsequently moved to Eastleigh as an Assistant Works Manager and later took a post at Derby. From here he then left the railway and after spending a few years working for an American mechanical engineering company in the UK moved careers to teach engineering. He was a complex character, volatile at times but also a most capable engineer. He never would achieve his youthful ambition to be a Chief Mechanical Engineer; he was simply in the wrong place at the wrong time. Indeed similar sentiments might even be said of his icon, Mr Bulleid, himself.

*Bulleid and the Turf Burner* by Ernest Shepherd, Kestrel Railway Books 2004.

**John Gaywood Click engrossed and smiling driving CC1. A steam man to the end.** *A. R. Pocklington*

# The Colour of the Southern

E arly in 2020 we were privileged to be able to acquire a collection of several hundred slides from a deceased enthusiast/photographer. I would also like to publicly thank Richard Halton of the *Medway Queen* Preservation Society for his help in securing the deal.

Most appear to have been taken in the 1960s with the occasional flashback to earlier times, and unfortunately with no list/index although the odd one does have some information on the slide mount. We hope you will enjoy this brief selection.

**Ramsgate just before the end of steam. Although there is no information on the slide, we can date this view from the presence of the BR Standard Class 5, No. 73042. This engine only came to the Southern Region on 14 June 1959, prior to this time having been on the London Midland. It was first allocated to Nine Elms but moved to Weymouth on 26 November 1959. It is probably fair to assume that it had thus been borrowed by Stewarts Lane and the photograph was therefore taken between June and November 1959. Alongside is No. 34085, at the time another Stewarts Lane engine but which moved west to Bournemouth in 1961. The support for the colour light signalling with the older semaphore tucked in behind will be noted.**

This time we have a date, September 1965; No. 34059 *Sir Archibald Sinclair,* named after the Secretary of State for Air in WW2, entering Dorchester South with a down (Weymouth) train. The engine is in the typical filthy condition as was virtually all steam at that time.

The one that was almost saved, No. 34057 *Biggin Hill*. This had been the selected engine the Bulleid Society had earmarked for preservation at the demise of steam on the Southern but it was withdrawn at the start of May 1967 a few weeks before the end, and a revision was made to No. 34023 *Blackmore Vale*. The engine is seen at Nine Elms, amongst the clutter and detritus of the steam depot in the course of terminal decline. From the white embellishments, railtour duty seems to have been a recent feature of its work, possibly the LCGB 'Bridport Belle' of 22 January 1967 or even the LCGB 'Hampshire Branch Lines' tour of 9 April 1967.

Moving east again we have a rear view of an unidentified interloper, A Western Rregion pannier tank, hard at work on the Folkestone Harbour branch in 1959, the first year WR engines were used on the branch. The identity of the engine is not reported.

Another semi-WR engine at work on the Southern. This is a BR Standard Class 3 tank, No. 82019, seen at Clapham Junction in May 1967. The design was very much an amalgam of LMS and GWR practice, the chassis being based on the LMS Ivatt Class 4 and the boiler on the Swindon No. 2 type as fitted to the 51xx and 56xx classes. All 45 were also built at Swindon. The class were split between the WR, SR, LMR and NER, those on the Southern ended up mainly being used from Nine Elms on carriage shunting and ECS trains from Waterloo – another type of modern tank engine the Southern had needed for some time. No. 82019 came new to the SR at Exmouth junction in September 1952 and lasted until the end of steam, by now at Nine Elms, in July 1967.

The Colour of the Southern

A wonderful action shot of one of the Ocean Liner special trains, this one being *The Statesman* service, we think near Vauxhall, sometime in 1963, no actual date, unfortunately. An (almost) all-Pullman boat train was slightly unusual although the number of luggage vans was commonplace. No one really travelled 'light' by liner. The engine is a presentable West Country, No. 34010 *Sidmouth,* with the first parcels van of Western Region Hawksworth type.

Station pilot duty for one of the last remaining M7 tank engines at Salisbury during a late spring snowfall in early 1963. No. 30034 certainly looks rundown, whilst the crew have done what they can to protect themselves from the elements, as witness the canvas sheet flapping from the cabside. This really was one of the last turns for this little engine which after a life just a couple of months short of 65 years was withdrawn in February 1963.

# The Colour of the Southern

No it is not a 'pull-push' with a Terrier. Instead a conventional Hayling train having just passed over Langston Harbour bridge, the latter's controlling signal box switched out, meaning the stop signals were cleared at either end. No date on this one but possibly out of the holiday season based on just the two-coach load.

*Opposite top:* **Sunshine at Nine Elms around October 1966. Another BR Class 3 tank, No. 82006, and this time displaying 'Swindon green' livery indicating perhaps an overhaul and a repaint at the Wiltshire works. Assuming the date to be correct the engine had been or was about to be withdrawn from service whilst alongside is Q1 No. 33009 which according to records had already been laid aside some months before. We must perhaps clarify that the date given for the image may not be 100% accurate. Both engines retain their coupling rods whilst some fire irons are leant against the footplate of the Q1. There also does not appear to be much rust showing on the wheels.**

*Bottom:* **Still in the London area, another Vauxhall shot and of a 'Schools' which we are told is No. 30934** *St. Lawrence,* **displaying to advantage its modified chimney below which is a multiple jet blast- pipe. The service is the 11.22 to Bournemouth on 8 September 1962.** *St. Lawrence* **was in the final months of service and succumbed at the end of December during the awful cull of steam that occurred on the Southern at that time.**

# Southern Staff

Every so often we come across odd items tucked in drawers or even files within other unrelated paperwork.

Such was the case here with three buff envelopes of Southern staff, some of whose names may just be familiar. If anyone can fill in any additional details we would be grateful.

We start with **William Henry Frank Mepsted**, M.Inst.T, some notes on whom first appeared in an unknown publication dated 16 October 1943. Accompanying an oval portrait as was customary at the time, we learn that Mr Mepsted had just been appointed Assistant to the Commercial Superintendent.

William Mepsted had begun his career as a junior clerk in the Goods Department at Deal in February 1912. After gaining further experience at Sandwich and on the relief staff, he entered the office of the Eastern District traffic superintendent at Ashford in 1914. From 1916 until 1919 he served in France and Belgium with the Railway Operating Division of the Royal Engineers. Upon his return to the railway he undertook various specialised duties, including control of the hop-picking traffic arrangements in the Paddock Wood area and the seasonal passenger traffic on the Kent coast.

After 1923 he joined the staff of the newly-appointed operating superintendent of the new Southern Division, at Brighton, as passenger trains' clerk, where he took part in the reconstruction of the Central Section passenger train timetable. Fifteen months later, in April 1925, he was appointed assistant Station Master at Victoria and became senior assistant Station Master there in May 1928.

In February 1933, he was made Station Master at Charing Cross, and in November 1936, assistant divisional superintendent, London East. In January 1942, he became divisional superintendent, Southern Division, Southampton, and was a member of the Poole Harbour Commission and the Southampton Port Emergency Committee while he held that post. Following his 1943 posting, in March 1949, he was appointed commercial superintendent, Southern Region, which post was subsequently re-designated as the chief commercial manager, and in October 1958, he took up the post of chief development officer, Southern Region. In the latter position 'Bill' Mepsted has organised an exhaustive survey of population trends in relation to future passenger service requirements and made a number of reports.

**William Henry Frank Mepsted in a portrait taken in 1942.**

Before the railways were nationalised and subsequently, he served on various inter-company and inter-regional conferences and committees dealing with commercial subjects. He was a member of the South Eastern Area Transport Users' Consultative Committee and a director of the Aldershot and District, Devon General, East Kent, Hants and Dorset, Maidstone and District, Southdown, and Wilts and Dorset bus undertakings. He retired from the Southern Region in April 1960.

**Yvonne Miles.** Nowadays, and rightly so, equal opportunities prevail but it was not so many years back when women were very much limited as to career prospects that might be available on the railway.

Little is known of Miss Miles, other than having a woman on the staff of the Chief Civil Engineer's department was clearly a novelty, hence the official photographer was sent out to record Yvonne at work – posed no doubt – on the trackside on 29 May 1968. Herewith is the limit of our available information but as before, if anyone can add further we would be delighted to include it in a future issue.

**'Jimmy' James.** Just the one view of Jimmy, reported as the manager at the Victoria Travel Centre when it opened on 25 October 1976. Save for this one image and one sentence written on the reverse of a print, this was what was contained in this envelope. Someone must remember 'Jimmy'?

*Above:* **Yvonne Miles.** Two of a small series of views taken, we may assume, in the Wimbledon area.

*Left:* **'Jimmy' James** of the Victoria Travel Centre.

# Stored Engines

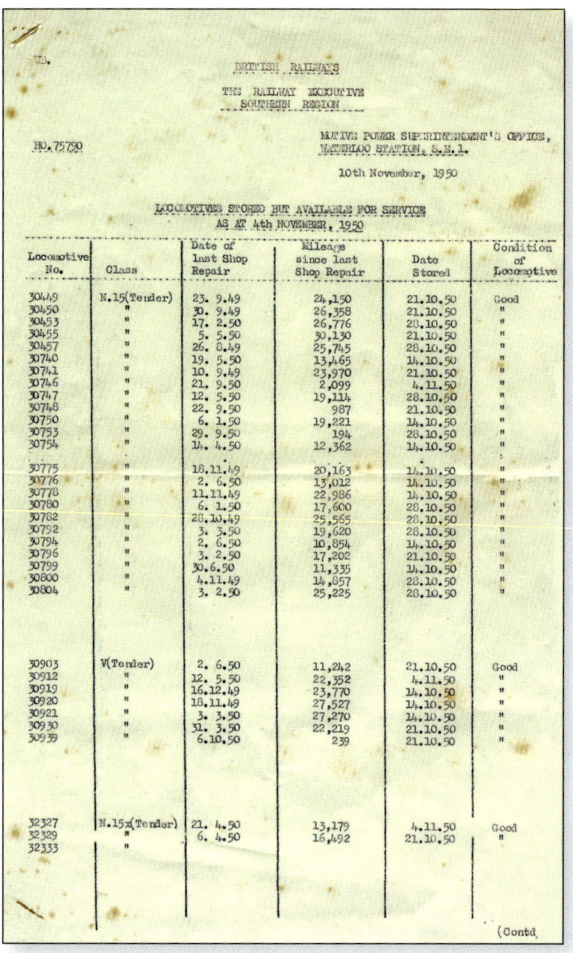

Facsimile of the first page of the original document.

Modern day railway operations dictate there is little spare capacity so far as surplus rolling stock is concerned. Indeed, I find it both amusing and sad that whilst starting to prepare this piece just before Christmas 2020 and the media are reporting that the Government have stated 'longer trains will be run in the lead up to the holiday.' Really? Has no one with any sense cottoned on that is just not possible with fixed formation sets? Perhaps what they really mean and should say is 'we will run extra trains,' but using what stock exactly?

In steam days and, to be fair, with contemporary electric units as well, there were usually some spare locomotives and rolling stock around – spare crews with the appropriate route knowledge might be another factor, though a steam depot could, usually, find a driver who'd signed for the route required. Spare coaching stock was invariably stored in various carriage sidings or even in what would otherwise be deserted sidings at some rural backwater, all ready to be brought into use either at short notice or in time for the resumption of holiday and summer traffic. It was in this way that the railway could deal with peaks – and troughs – of traffic, the very thing Dr Beeching was later determined to get rid of and so reduce the amount of time an expensive asset might otherwise sit depreciating without being used.

Other than simply referring to the subject of stored rolling stock, this article will, as the title suggests, concentrate on stored locomotives and we should remember without any rose-tinted spectacles, the steam locomotive was not a totally predictable machine and a fault reported by a driver could mean it might not therefore be available to take up its next scheduled duty. Add to this that not all engines working on the Southern were fitted with TIA water treatment and consequently boiler washouts were commonplace, meaning an engine could therefore be out of service perhaps as often as one day in seven. In addition there were the necessary regular scheduled examinations and the like.

# Stored Engines

**L1 No. 31786 (which also featured in the 1950 list) together with another of the same class, plus a few more locos in a line at Bricklayers Arms on 28 April 1951. No. 31786 was noted by the photographer as being malachite green and with the smokebox door missing. Other locos noted at 'The Brick' on that day were 'Cs' Nos. 31071 and 31227. Bricklayers Arms seems to have been one of those locations regularly used for storing engines. It is possible No. 31786 had been in store from at least November 1950 to April 1960 but it did work again and survived until February 1962.** *Ted West/Mike King collection*

Consequently each large depot was, within its allocation, supposed to have sufficient stock of engines of various power types to provide spare capacity to cover all the duties required to be worked and also extra trains when needed. Even so, during times of peak demand, it was still sometimes the case of scraping the bottom of the barrel to find suitable power. Digressing slightly, there is the lovely tale applicable I think to Bath (S&D) when a driver arriving for duty discovered his expected engine was not available and instead had been allocated something far less suitable and with a poor reputation. On complaining to the foreman, said individual was most apologetic and appeared to relent commenting, 'OK, take any engine you like in the shed.' The driver, suitably relieved, strode into the shed to find – just two: his own regular engine under repair and the solitary less suitable alternative. (An object lesson in how to become a Foreman!)

To return to our topic in hand, it follows that there were times when there might be a surfeit of engines, which might then be stored. Basically spare for the period and most likely at the end of the summer timetable and before the demand had risen again, in the lead-up to Christmas, and again after that and prior to the start of the following year's summer service.

On occasions reports of stored engines have appeared in various publications, the *Railway Observer* being very good at this type of information. And whilst not in any way wishing to doubt these accounts, what follows is the very first time we have ever seen any original paperwork affording this type of information.

The original document, running to no less than seven foolscap pages, shows the situation 'as at 4 November 1950' and is signed for (by) T. E. Chrimes, the Southern Region Motive Power Superintendent at Waterloo. The actual heading is 'Locomotives Stored but available for Service.' The document is dated 10 November so we can imagine the request had gone out some days earlier to all depots to report the situation as existed on 4 November. The paperwork thus indicates a most interesting 'dip check' on that one day with much ancillary information but lacks just one point which today we might have found useful – where were these engines stored – which depots?

Another question might be 'why'? But this is probably more simply answered as the late autumn of 1950 was a time when coal was in short supply; and so it is likely that included in the normal tally of engines that might be stored were those temporarily without work due to trains cancelled due to shortage of fuel.

In order to maintain strict accuracy we have deliberately not attempted to collate engine numbers to depots. Unfortunately being foolscap it is also not possible to reproduce the originals with total accuracy on SW page size and in consequence we present a facsimile of the first page with the whole information otherwise reported below in table form and in the class/number order they appear in the listing, which is not the originating company or designer order. It will quickly be noted that there is a greater percentage of former LSWR Drummond 4-4-0 types than any other.

Note: The depot the locomotive was allocated to on 31-8-50 is shown in the right hand column, but this information was not included on the original paperwork and is instead taken from the *Ian Allan ABC Supplement Loco-Shed Book Pt. 2 Southern Regions* and was reported as accurate on 31 August 1950. Some change of depots may therefore have taken place between 31 August and 4 November but it is as accurate as we can make it. It is for this reason that the information in this column is also shown in italics. It is reasonable to assume that in the majority of cases engines would also have been stored at their home depots.

| Locomotive No. | Class | Date of Last Shop Repair | Mileage Since Last Shop Repair | Date Stored | Condition of Locomotive | *Allocation as at 31-8-50* |
|---|---|---|---|---|---|---|
| 30449 | N.15 (Tender) | 23-9-49 | 24,150 | 21-10-50 | Good | *72B* |
| 30450 | N.15 (Tender) | 30-9-49 | 26,359 | 21-10-50 | Good | *72B* |
| 30453 | N.15 (Tender) | 17-2-50 | 26,776 | 28-10-50 | Good | *72B* |
| 30455 | N.15 (Tender) | 5-5-50 | 30,10 | 21-10-50 | Good | *72A* |
| 30457 | N.15 (Tender) | 26-8-49 | 25,745 | 28-10-50 | Good | *72A* |
| 30740 | N.15 (Tender) | 19-9-50 | 13,465 | 14-10-50 | Good | *71B* |
| 30741 | N.15 (Tender) | 10-9-49 | 23,970 | 21-10-50 | Good | *71B* |
| 30746 | N.15 (Tender) | 21-9-50 | 2,099 | 4-11-50 | Good | *71B* |
| 30747 | N.15 (Tender) | 12-5-50 | 19,114 | 28-10-50 | Good | *70A* |
| 30748 | N.15 (Tender) | 22-9-50 | 987 | 21-10-50 | Good | *72B* |
| 30750 | N.15 (Tender) | 5-1-50 | 19,221 | 14-10-50 | Good | *71B* |
| 30753 | N.15 (Tender) | 29-9-50 | 194 | 28-10-50 | Good | *72B* |
| 30754 | N.15 (Tender) | 14-4-50 | 12,362 | 14-10-50 | Good | *71B* |
| 30775 | N.15 (Tender) | 18-11-49 | 20,163 | 14-10-50 | Good | *73A* |
| 30776 | N.15 (Tender) | 2-6-50 | 13,012 | 14-10-50 | Good | *73A* |
| 30778 | N.15 (Tender) | 11-11-49 | 22,986 | 14-10-50 | Good | *73A* |
| 30780 | N.15 (Tender) | 6-1-50 | 17,600 | 28-10-50 | Good | *70A* |
| 30782 | N.15 (Tender) | 26-10-49 | 25,565 | 28-10-50 | Good | *70A* |
| 30792 | N.15 (Tender) | 3-3-50 | 19,620 | 28-10-50 | Good | *70A* |
| 30794 | N.15 (Tender) | 2-6-50 | 10,854 | 14-10-50 | Good | *73B* |
| 30796 | N.15 (Tender) | 3-2-50 | 17,202 | 21-10-50 | Good | *73A* |
| 30799 | N.15 (Tender) | 30-6-50 | 11,335 | 14-10-50 | Good | *73B* |
| 30800 | N.15 (Tender) | 4-11-49 | 14,857 | 28-10-50 | Good | *73C* |
| 30804 | N.15 (Tender) | 3-2-50 | 25,225 | 28-10-50 | Good | *74A* |
| 30903 | V (Tender) | 2-6-50 | 11,242 | 21-10-50 | Good | *74E* |
| 30912 | V (Tender) | 12-5-50 | 22,352 | 4-11-50 | Good | *74B* |
| 30919 | V (Tender) | 16-12-40 | 23,770 | 14-10-50 | Good | *73B* |
| 30920 | V (Tender) | 18-11-49 | 27,527 | 14-10-50 | Good | *73B* |
| 30921 | V (Tender) | 3-3-50 | 27,270 | 14-10-50 | Good | *73B* |
| 30930 | V (Tender) | 31-3-50 | 22,219 | 21-10-50 | Good | *73B* |
| 30939 | V (Tender) | 6-10-50 | 239 | 21-10-50 | Good | *73B* |
| 32327 | N.15x (Tender) | 21-4-50 | 13,179 | 4-11-50 | Good | *70D* |
| 32329 | N.15x (Tender) | 6-4-50 | 16,492 | 21-10-50 | Good | *70D* |
| 32333 | N.15x (Tender) | – | – | – | – | *70D* |
| 32425 | H.2 (Tender) | 6-10-50 | – | 4-11-50 | Good | *75A (Newhaven)* |
| 32043 | B.4x (Tender) | 2-10-48 | 1,928 | 13-11-48 | Good | *75G* |
| 32045 | B.4x (Tender) | 9-2-46 | 6,356 | 29-7-50 | Good | *70G* |

# Stored Engines

T9 No. (30)303 at Fratton, with similar stored examples either side. Fratton has also gone to the trouble of adding sacking to the tops of the chimney, a recognisable sign the engines were indeed in store. Interestingly the Waterloo paperwork refers to all the stored engines with their BR '30' suffix even as in this case (and several others) the number allocated was not actually carried. It was reported as having been in good condition and had run 24,159 miles since its last repair.

| | | | | | | |
|---|---|---|---|---|---|---|
| 32050 | B.4x (Tender) | 15-12-45 | 23,992 | 31-12-50 | Good | *73B* |
| 32052 | B.4x (Tender) | 19-7-47 | 13,503 | 29-7-50 | Good | *70D* |
| 32055 | B.4x (Tender) | 21-1-46 | 12,926 | 22-7-50 | Good | *75G* |
| 32056 | B.4x (Tender) | 21-2-44 | 98,245 | 18-2-50 | Fair | *73B* |
| 32060 | B.4x (Tender) | 6-3-48 | 20,679 | 5-8-50 | Good | *75G* |
| 32067 | B.4x (Tender) | 16-2-46 | 3,246 | 29-7-50 | Good | *70D* |
| 32070 | B.4x (Tender) | 11-1-47 | 17,919 | 31-12-50 | Good | *73B* |
| 32071 | B.4x (Tender) | 24-11-45 | 67,946 | 22-7-50 | Moderate | *75G* |
| 32072 | B.4x (Tender) | 10-2-50 | 1,324 | 5-8-50 | Good | *75G* |
| 32073 | B.4x (Tender) | 2-11-46 | 48,286 | 31-12-49 | Moderate | *75G* |
| 30463 (oil) | D.15 (Tender) | 20-9-47 | 26,353 | 9-10-48 | Good | *71A* |
| 30464 | D.15 (Tender) | 21-4-50 | – | 6-5-50 | Good | *71A* |
| 30467 | D.15 (Tender) | 6-10-50 | – | 14-10-50 | Good | *71A* |
| 32037 | H.1 (Tender) | 6-9-45 | 71,183 | 14-10-50 | Fair | *75A (Newhaven)* |
| 32038 | H.1 (Tender) | 13-9-47 | 36,511 | 7-10-50 | Good | *75A (Newhaven)* |
| 32039 | H.1 (Tender) | 22-10-42 | 105,386 | 10-9-49 | Fair | *75A* |
| 31345 | D.1 (Tender) | 8-12-49 | 15,831 | 21-10-50 | Good | *71A* |
| 31736 | D.1 (Tender) | 23-4-49 | 15,157 | 24-6-50 | Good | *74A* |
| 31019 | E.1 (Tender) | 18-5-50 | 11,090 | 14-10-50 | Good | *73A* |
| 31067 | E.1 (Tender) | 28-4-50 | 12,941 | 21-10-50 | Good | *73A* |
| 31762 | L (Tender) | 14-7-49 | 13,079 | 14-10-50 | Good | *73A* |
| 31764 | L (Tender) | 9-7-49 | 19,342 | 14-10-50 | Good | *73A* |
| 31767 | L (Tender) | 10-7-48 | 26,898 | 14-10-50 | Good | *73A* |

| 31773 | L (Tender) | 8-10-49 | 25,799 | 28-10-50 | Good | 74A |
|---|---|---|---|---|---|---|
| 31776 | L (Tender) | 17-9-49 | 19,752 | 14-10-50 | Good | 74B |
| 31781 | L (Tender) | 26-7-50 | 8,865 | 21-10-50 | Good | 74B |
| 31756 | L.1 (Tender) | 5-6-48 | 29,134 | 14-10-50 | Good | 74C |
| 31757 | L.1 (Tender) | 2-6-50 | 11,497 | 14-10-50 | Good | 74C |
| 31782 | L.1 (Tender) | 24-9-49 | 14,478 | 4-11-50 | Good | 73B |
| 31784 | L.1 (Tender) | 11-9-48 | 26,948 | 14-10-50 | Good | 73B |
| 31786 | L.1 (Tender) | 24-7-48 | 27,220 | 14-10-50 | Good | 73B |
| 31787 | L.1 (Tender) | 22-10-49 | 21,314 | 21-10-50 | Good | 73B |
| 30415 | L.12 (Tender) | 6-1-50 | 5,536 | 21-10-50 | Good | 71C |
| 30416 | L.12 (Tender) | 7-5-49 | 19,083 | 4-11-50 | Good | 70C |
| 30426 | L.12 (Tender) | 21-10-49 | 13,428 | 21-10-50 | Good | 71D |
| 30427 | L.12 (Tender) | 7-10-49 | 10,270 | 14-10-50 | Good | 71D |
| 30430 | L.12 (Tender) | 22-11-47 | 25,868 | 18-2-50 | Good | 71A |
| 30431 | L.12 (Tender) | 15-5-49 | 36,064 | 11-2-50 | Good | 71A |
| 30434 | L.12 (Tender) | 3-3-50 | 2,590 | 29-4-50 | Good | 71A |
| 30396 | S.11 (Tender) | 23-10-48 | 18,183 | 28-10-50 | Good | 71D |
| 30397 | S.11 (Tender) | 25-6-49 | 15,151 | 28-10-50 | Good | 71D |
| 30398 | S.11 (Tender) | 28-4-50 | 9,887 | 29-7-50 | Good | 71B |
| 30399 | S.11 (Tender) | 12-6-48 | 17,570 | 21-10-50 | Good | 71C |
| 30400 | S.11 (Tender) | 24-2-50 | 214 | 18-3-50 | Good | 71D |

**Another New Cross Gate stored engine, this time between November 1948 and February 1949, was this B4X No. 2052 – by November 1950 it was reported as in store at Basingstoke which might seem an unusual location – paper transfer perhaps? It later moved to Eastbourne. Whether it ever worked much after 1950 is doubtful as it was withdrawn in December 1951.** *R. C. Riley/The Transport Treasury*

## Stored Engines

| | | | | | | |
|---|---|---|---|---|---|---|
| 30401 | S.11 (Tender) | 23-11-47 | 31,668 | 29-4-50 | Good | 71A |
| 30113 (oil) | T.9 (Tender) | 20-9-47 | 31,324 | 9-10-48 | Good | 71D |
| 30114 (oil) | T.9 (Tender) | 6-9-47 | 19,531 | 9-10-48 | Good | 71D |
| 30115 (oil) | T.9 (Tender) | 29-6-46 | 52,469 | 2-10-48 | Moderate | 71D |
| 30118 (oil) | T.9 (Tender) | 1-9-45 | 92,077 | 9-10-48 | Fair | 71D |
| 30119 | T.9 (Tender) | 1-5-48 | 27,805 | 19-8-50 | Good | 70A |
| 30120 | T.9 (Tender) | 9-6-50 | 6,048 | 12-8-50 | – | 71D |
| 30121 (oil) | T.9 (Tender) | 27-6-45 | 83,297 | 9-10-48 | Fair | 71A |
| 30280 (oil) | T.9 (Tender) | 13-9-47 | 22,432 | 9-10-48 | Good | 71D |
| 30283 | T.9 (Tender) | 19-2-49 | 23,287 | 14-10-50 | Good | 72A |
| 30286 (oil) | T.9 (Tender) | 15-9-45 | 72,939 | 9-10-48 | Fair | 71A |
| 30287 | T.9 (Tender) | 21-4-50 | – | 6-5-50 | Good | 71A |
| 30289 | T.9 (Tender) | 29-9-50 | 100 | 14-10-50 | Good | 72B |
| 30301 | T.9 (Tender) | 23-9-49 | 8,515 | 25-2-50 | Good | 72B |
| 30303 (oil) | T.9 (Tender) | 20-9-47 | 24,159 | 9-10-48 | Good | 71D |
| 30305 (oil) | T.9 (Tender) | 23-11-46 | 31,458 | 9-10-48 | Good | 71D |
| 30310 | T.9 (Tender) | 2-8-50 | 369 | 26-8-50 | Good | 71D |
| 30313 | T.9 (Tender) | 4-6-49 | 16,475 | 14-10-50 | Good | 71A |
| 30314 (oil) | T.9 (Tender) | 13-9-47 | 32,237 | 9-10-48 | Good | 71D |
| 30336 | T.9 (Tender) | 5-5-50 | 8,462 | 28-10-50 | Good | 70C |

**For the purposes of this article, please ignore No. 36001; stored she might well be but as referred to in the text this engine was not included, as she was never taken into capital stock. Instead the focus should really be on the engines behind, the N15 and particularly the H15, as this was one of the stored members of the H15 class reported as at Eastleigh in November.**

One of two O1 0-6-0 engines stored at New Cross Gate in November 1950 and still in store ten months later on 25 September 1951 but this time at Hither Green. The only difference is that by the latter date it had been withdrawn (June 1951) and so may even have ceased work before November 1950.
*R. E. Vincent/The Transport Treasury*

| 30338 | T.9 (Tender) | 18-8-50 | 1,530 | 23-9-50 | Good | 71C |
|---|---|---|---|---|---|---|
| 30703 | T.9 (Tender) | 9-7-49 | 17,690 | 21-10-50 | Good | 72A |
| 30705 | T.9 (Tender) | 21-5-49 | 6,568 | 29-4-50 | Good | 71A |
| 30706 | T.9 (Tender) | 3-9-49 | 14,566 | 14-10-50 | Good | 72A |
| 30708 | T.9 (Tender) | 5-3-49 | 12,551 | 29-4-50 | Good | 71A |
| 30709 | T.9 (Tender) | 28-4-50 | 72 | 13-5-50 | Good | 72B |
| 30710 | T.9 (Tender) | 5-8-49 | 17,160 | 28-10-50 | Good | 70C |
| 30711 | T.9 (Tender) | 21-5-49 | 7,483 | 29-4-50 | Good | 71A |
| 30713 (oil) | T.9 (Tender) | 6-9-47 | 13,303 | 9-10-48 | Good | 71A |
| 30715 | T.9 (Tender) | 10-3-50 | 8,419 | 14-10-50 | Good | 72A |
| 30718 | T.9 (Tender) | 17-4-48 | 22,979 | 28-10-50 | Good | 70A |
| 30719 | T.9 (Tender) | 25-6-49 | 9,948 | 19-8-50 | Good | 72B |
| 30721 | T.9 (Tender) | 23-7-49 | 2,725 | 29-4-50 | Good | 71A |
| 30722 (oil) | T.9 (Tender) | 24-10-46 | 36,126 | 9-10-48 | Good | 71A |
| 30724 | T.9 (Tender) | 23-7-49 | 12,367 | 12-8-50 | Good | 72B |
| 30727 | T.9 (Tender) | 10-2-50 | 6,207 | 22-4-50 | Good | 72B |
| 30729 | T.9 (Tender) | 11-12-48 | 13,806 | 19-8-50 | Good | 71A |
| 30731 (oil) | T.9 (Tender) | 30-8-47 | 19,586 | 9-10-48 | Good | 71D |
| 30732 | T.9 (Tender) | 17-9-49 | 10,573 | 29-4-50 | Good | 70B |
| 31488 | D (Tender) | 24-3-50 | 13,254 | 14-10-50 | Good | 73B |
| 31490 | D (Tender) | 22-5-48 | 33,107 | 16-9-50 | Good | 73B |
| 31501 | D (Tender) | 21-4-50 | 8,029 | 4-11-50 | Good | 73E |
| 31586 | D (Tender) | 5-6-48 | 24,008 | 19-8-50 | Good | 73E |

| | | | | | | |
|---|---|---|---|---|---|---|
| 31591 | D (Tender) | 3-2-50 | 2,278 | 14-10-50 | Good | *73B* |
| 31729 | D (Tender) | 20-1-50 | 4,111 | 14-10-50 | Good | *73D* |
| 31732 | D (Tender) | 12-11-47 | 33,102 | 12-8-50 | Good | *73C* |
| 31734 | D (Tender) | 21-7-50 | 746 | 12-8-50 | Good | *73E* |
| 31737 | D (Tender) | 25-9-48 | 19,621 | 14-10-50 | Good | *74C* |
| 31744 | D (Tender) | 29-10-49 | 24,321 | 21-10-50 | Good | *70E* |
| 31746 | D (Tender) | 28-4-50 | 1,771 | 14-10-50 | Good | *73B* |
| 31166 | E (Tender) | 19-6-48 | 8,323 | 14-10-50 | Good | *73B* |
| 31175 | E (Tender) | 14-11-47 | 8,445 | 31-12-49 | Good | *73B* |
| 31273 | E (Tender) | 24-9-49 | 24,398 | 14-10-50 | Good | *73B* |
| 31315 | E (Tender) | 7-8-48 | 8,160 | 7-1-50 | Good | *73B* |
| 31491 | E (Tender) | 7-2-48 | 5,387 | 31-12-49 | Good | *73B* |
| 32075 | I.3 (Tank) | 30-9-49 | 27,552 | 21-10-50 | Good | *75F* |
| 32091 | I.3 (Tank) | 16-12-49 | 1,288 | 29-7-50 | Good | *75E* |
| 31265 | H (Tank) | 19-2-49 | 40,382 | 15-7-50 | Moderate | *74B* |
| 31278 | H (Tank) | 21-10-49 | 3,882 | 14-10-50 | Good | *73B* |
| 31309 | H (Tank) | 20-1-50 | 1,570 | 18-2-50 | Good | *73B* |
| 31328 | H (Tank) | 23-4-49 | 15,186 | 28-10-50 | Good | *74E* |
| 31500 | H (Tank) | 5-5-50 | 4,225 | 5-8-50 | Good | *73B* |
| 31530 | H (Tank) | 19-2-50 | 7,299 | 5-8-50 | Good | *74C* |
| 31661 | R (Tank) | 12-2-49 | 24,197 | 4-11-50 | Good | *73E* |
| 31674 | R (Tank) | 12-2-49 | 23,021 | 4-11-50 | Good | *73E* |
| 31708 | R.1 (Tank) | 4-10-46 | 22,911 | 1-4-50 | Good | *74C* |
| 30192 | O.2 (Tank) | 18-8-50 | 1,047 | 14-10-50 | Good | *72A* |
| 30230 | O.2 (Tank) | 16-6-50 | 3,714 | 14-10-50 | Good | *72A* |
| 32644 | A.1x (Tank) | 24-7-48 | 18,449 | 14-10-50 | Good | *74A* |
| 32646 | A.1x (Tank) | 29-9-49 | 12,679 | 17-6-50 | Good | *71D* |
| 32659 | A.1x (Tank) | 31-3-50 | 1,672 | 14-10-50 | Good | *74A* |
| 32677 | A.1x (Tank) | 6-8-49 | 6,717 | 7-10-50 | Good | *71D* |
| 32678 | A.1x (Tank) | 25-10-45 | 49,204 | 14-10-50 | Moderate | *74A* |
| 30475 | H.15 (Tender) | 16-10-48 | 38,673 | 12-8-50 | Good | *71A* |
| 30483 | H.15 (Tender) | 11-8-50 | – | 19-8-50 | Good | *71A* |
| 30489 | H.15 (Tender) | 8-9-50 | – | 9-9-50 | Good | *71A* |
| 30491 | H.15 (Tender) | 22-9-50 | 501 | 7-10-50 | Good | *71A* |
| 30523 | H.15 (Tender) | 23-7-49 | 12,189 | 14-10-50 | Good | *71A* |
| 31615 | U (Tender) | 8-9-50 | 3,153 | 4-11-50 | Good | *70A* |
| 31625 | U (Tender) | 22-9-50 | 579 | 21-10-50 | Good | *70A* |
| 32399 | E.5 (Tank) | 21-10-49 | 1,299 | 14-10-50 | Good | *75D* |
| 32406 | E.5 (Tank) | 3-9-49 | 20,634 | 23-9-50 | Good | *75G* |
| 32568 | E.5 (Tank) | 3-7-48 | 3,026 | 14-10-50 | Good | *75D* |
| 32571 | E.5 (Tank) | 21-8-48 | 7,350 | 31-12-49 | Good | *75E* |
| 32573 | E.5 (Tank) | 19-7-47 | 28,017 | 21-10-50 | Good | *75A* |
| 32585 | E.5 (Tank) | 30-12-49 | 15,850 | 2-9-50 | Good | *73B (New Cross)* |
| 32587 | E.5 (Tank) | 10-3-50 | 11,875 | 9-9-50 | Good | *73B (New Cross)* |
| 32588 | E.5 (Tank) | 18-11-49 | 268 | 3-12-49 | Good | *75G* |
| 32590 | E.5 (Tank) | 14-5-49 | 2,836 | 14-1-50 | Good | *73B* |
| 32591 | E.5 (Tank) | 1-12-49 | 1,241 | 31-12-49 | Good | *75G* |
| 32592 | E.5 (Tank) | 8-1-47 | 68,514 | 14-10-50 | Good | *75B* |
| 32595 | E.5 (Tank) | 13-1-50 | 12,029 | 9-9-59 | Good | *75A* |
| W3 | E.1 (Tank) | 23-12-44 | 77,252 | 14-10-50 | Good | *71E* |
| 31041 | O.1 (Tender) | 29-3-47 | 50,719 | 25-3-50 | Moderate | *74A* |
| 31044 | O.1 (Tender) | 14-1-48 | 52,821 | 1-4-50 | Moderate | *73B* |

| | | | | | | |
|---|---|---|---|---|---|---|
| 31064 | O.1 (Tender) | 3-5-47 | 70,732 | 1-4-50 | Fair | *73B (New Cross)* |
| 31065 | O.1 (Tender) | 28-2-48 | 41,021 | 1-4-50 | Moderate | *74B* |
| 31066 | O.1 (Tender) | 15-3-47 | 56,124 | 1-4-50 | Moderate | *73B (New Cross)* |
| 31093 | O.1 (Tender) | 16-12-47 | 50,737 | 1-4-50 | Moderate | *74B* |
| 31108 | O.1 (Tender) | 20-12-46 | 64,471 | 1-4-50 | Moderate | *74C* |
| 31248 | O.1 (Tender) | 8-9-44 | 103,687 | 1-4-50 | Fair | *73C* |
| 31258 | O.1 (Tender) | 19-7-47 | 48,015 | 23-3-50 | Moderate | *73C* |
| 31369 | O.1 (Tender) | 10-9-47 | 68,264 | 1-4-50 | Moderate | *73E* |
| 31373 | O.1 (Tender) | 30-1-48 | 43,170 | 24-6-50 | Moderate | *74C* |
| 31379 | O.1 (Tender) | 28-9-46 | 84,318 | 25-3-50 | Fair | *74A* |
| 31381 | O.1 (Tender) | 5-12-45 | 78,142 | 25-3-50 | Fair | *74C* |
| 31383 ex KESR | O.1 (Tender) | 12-4-35 | 30,473 | 14-10-50 | Moderate | *74C* |
| 31390 | O.1 (Tender) | 21-10-46 | 58,355 | 8-4-50 | Moderate | *74B* |
| 31391 | O.1 (Tender) | 8-11-47 | 58,565 | 1-4-50 | Moderate | *73C* |
| 31395 | O.1 (Tender) | 11-12-47 | 55,912 | 25-3-50 | Moderate | *73B (New Cross)* |
| 31432 | O.1 (Tender) | 5-10-46 | 62,142 | 1-4-50 | Moderate | *73C* |
| 32054 | B.4 (Tender) | 17-8-43 | 25,063 | 13-4-46 | Good | *75G* |
| 32062 | B.4 (Tender) | 21-2-44 | 41,397 | 6-4-46 | Fair | *75G* |
| 32063 | B.4 (Tender) | 11-9-40 | 27,616 | 6-4-46 | Moderate | *75G* |
| 32068 | B.4 (Tender) | 20-3-39 | 41,919 | 20-4-46 | Moderate | *75G* |
| 32005 | I.1x (Tank) | 3-3-48 | 505 | 31-12-49 | Good | *75A* |

**This time it is R1 No. 31698 that is seen out of use at Tonbridge and a few years later in May 1955. Only one member of the class was noted as stored in November 1950. Again it was in its last months of 'formal' listing and was condemned in October 1955.** *Eric Sawford/The Transport Treasury*

| | | | | | | |
|---|---|---|---|---|---|---|
| 32008 | I.1x (Tank) | 1-3-47 | 32,166 | 8-1-49 | Moderate | *73B (New Cross)* |
| 32009 | I.1x (Tank) | 10-11-45 | 44,416 | 1-1-49 | Good | *75G* |
| 32595 | I.1x (Tank) | 13-9-47 | 11,277 | 10-5-48 | Good | *75A* |
| 32596 | I.1x (Tank) | 25-4-47 | 36,508 | 31-12-49 | Moderate | *73B (New Cross)* |
| 32602 | I.1x (Tank) | 3-2-45 | 46,691 | 8-1-49 | Moderate | *73B* |
| 32603 | I.1x (Tank) | 17-4-46 | 31,425 | 8-1-49 | Moderate | *75G* |
| 30148 (oil) | L.11 (Tender) | 27-9-47 | 13,147 | 21-8-48 | Good | *71A* |
| 30154 (oil) | L.11 (Tender) | 17-8-46 | 34,280 | 9-10-48 | Fair | *71A* |
| 30155 (oil) | L.11 (Tender) | 17-8-46 | 31,709 | 9-10-48 | Fair | *71A* |
| 30157 (oil) | L.11 (Tender) | 11-10-47 | 17,104 | 21-8-48 | Good | *71A* |
| 30170 (oil) | L.11 (Tender) | 4-10-47 | 13,343 | 9-10-48 | Good | *71D* |
| 30172 (oil) | L.11 (Tender) | 27-9-47 | 16,638 | 9-10-48 | Good | *71D* |
| 30411 (oil) | L.11 (Tender) | 23-8-47 | 14,734 | 9-10-48 | Good | *71A* |
| 30437 (oil) | L.11 (Tender) | 24-7-47 | 8,808 | 21-8-48 | Good | *71A* |
| 30442 | L.11 (Tender) | 25-9-48 | 11,519 | 14-10-48 | Good | *71A* |

A brief reminder also of the shed codes quoted:

| | | | | |
|---|---|---|---|---|
| 70A Nine Elms | 71A Eastleigh | 72A Exmouth Junc. | 73A Stewarts Lane | 74A Ashford | 75A Brighton |
| 70C Guildford | 71B Bournemouth | 72B Salisbury | 73B Bricklayers Arms/ New Cross Gate | 74B Ramsgate | 75D Horsham |
| 70D Basingstoke | 71D Fratton | | 73C Hither Green | 74C Dover/Folkestone | 75F Tunbridge Wells |
| 70E Reading | | | 73D Gillingham | 74E Three Bridges | 75G Eastbourne |
| | | | 73E Faversham | | |

Note: Only those sheds that are relevant are shown.

**In the same year, on 8 November 1955, No. 30750 *Morgan le Fay* was reported as 'stored in ex-works condition' at Eastleigh. As with many of the class, inroads were being made into their numbers in the 1950s in consequence of the input of so many Standard and Bulleid types. No. 30750 would only last until June 1957.**

The low mileage since works attention of certain engines, Nos. 30748, 30750, 30939, 30400, 30310, 30707, 31734, 30491, 31625, 32588 and 32005, will also be noted. It might have been expected that engines with a higher mileage would have been the ones to have been stood down.

In addition we might draw attention to the two years the oil burners had been stored and yet still regarded as in good condition; none would ever steam again. Other engines, particularly some examples of the B.4 tender class, had been stored from as long back as 1946.

An interesting exercise is also to consider for a moment a couple of example classes. The N15 class for example where no less than 24 out of 74 engines, just under one third of the class, were stored. Another modern class with a fairly high percentage out of use were the Schools, 7 out of 40.

Another query concerns the members of the 'Schools' – six from Bricklayers Arms, which was their normal London shed for the Kent Coast and Hastings services – but the last is at Three Bridges – NOT a shed where you would usually find a 'Schools'. It would be tempting to say the odd one at Three Bridges was awaiting Works, but with her mileage, it would be more likely to be for a repair of something busted, rather than a routine maintenance. At this time, 30903 *Charterhouse* was usually employed on the Hastings line.

We would need further detail to accurately explain the full details of the list; might some engines simply be awaiting works attention (but the paperwork heading tends to imply not) and was this as much a paper exercise rather than to indicate the works had longer waiting lists than was desirable? Similarly those with low mileage could even represent examples where adjustments had been found necessary and this too was awaited.

Having certain older types being in store is perhaps more easily explained whilst it will also be seen, with the T9 class for example, that some engines were stored following the abortive oil-firing episode. As we know, these would never be restored to use.

So did the Southern really have so many engines that were not required? Well, we should remember this was the era of the Bulleid Pacifics, by this date nearly 140 in service and in

**D1 No. 31247 and L1 No. 31784 out of use at Redhill on 18 October 1959. At the time both were officially allocated to Nine Elms, and had been since June 1959. It is possible the latter shed simply did not want or did not have room for them.** *R.C. Riley/The Transport Treasury*

# Stored Engines

Latter day storage, in this case D1 No. 31246, heading a line of similar engines at Feltham on 2 August 1959. This was just one of numerous steam engines displaced as a result of Phase 1 of the Kent Coast electrification and in the case of No. 31246 moved west to Nine Elms with effect from 14 June 1959. Either Nine Elms did not want it, or had no work for it, or perhaps considered it not in good enough condition and consequently it and several sisters were instead sent to Feltham for store. Why to Feltham? Well that may have been simply due to space constraints at Nine Elms. We cannot be certain what work it may, or may not, have subsequently undertaken, as records show the engine was withdrawn on 11 March 1961. In general terms engines might be stored for several reasons; simply awaiting their next duty, awaiting a works visit, or as in later times, withdrawn and awaiting the call to scrap. Other reasons could be simple lack of work consequent upon more modern replacement motive power or line closures. Two members of the D1 class were reported as stored in November 1950 but No. 31246 was not one of them.

consequence there would have been a cascade effect which might go to explain why so many N15s especially were not working. (It will be seen no Bulleid engines were included in the list.) It would also not be long before a literal avalanche of Standard types would start to descend on the Southern meaning older engines still stored might in fact never be restored to traffic.

A second document, if it were ever available, showing the same situation perhaps dated 1953 or 1954, would make for an interesting comparison.

Two last comments of fact to conclude. Firstly, Leader No. 36001 is not shown, even though the engine was not (quite) officially condemned at this time. The omission simply meant that it had never been taken into capital stock. However its predecessor No. 32039 (the sleeve-valve converted Atlantic) was included, even if against the entry for No. 32039 it was shown as only being in 'Fair' condition and had in fact already been stored since September 1949.

# Rebuilt
## The Letters and Comments Pages

We start this month with a note from **Tony Francis** on the image on p. 27 of *SW51* (the article dealt with the runaway from Caterham to Selhurst, by Nicholas Owen). Tony is able to identify the Gentleman standing on the rails and looking up into the cab as Pete Bailey. 'Pete was a fitter in steam days at Stewarts Lane and later Foreman and Crane Supervisor in the Electric Loco shed there. It is in his capacity as crane supervisor that he is at Norwood Junction trying to sort out the mess. When not dealing with incidents such as this, Pete was involved in preparing locos for Royals and other special trips; the Class 73s in the 1970s used to look superb including fitting the specially burnished buffers. The latter were kept on a pallet in the stores when not required on a locomotive. Pete used to ride with the loco on most VIP trips which led him to remark to me that he also went on honeymoon with Charles and Diana!'

*Above and opposite page:* Two recently unearthed images of the Strowger-Hudd Automatic Control System that was tested on short sections of the Southern, LMS and LNER. Unlike the widespread contact system of ATC used on the GWR, there was no physical contact between the ramp and a 'shoe' on the locomotive, the system instead working by magnetic induction. Operationally there was similarity to the GWR ATC system, namely if the distant signal is clear a short blast is given on the hooter fitted to the locomotive; a useful adjunct to this being that it also helped give the driver confirmation as to his whereabouts in poor weather. Should the distant signal be 'on' then a longer blast was given and unless acknowledged by the driver, the brakes were applied. Where the system differed from that of the GWR was that a prolonged blast was also given in advance on the approach to a stop signal which was at 'on' and the brakes applied. On the Southern at least one 'King Arthur' locomotive was equipped for test purposes whilst we believe the actual trackside equipment was set up on a short section of the former LSWR main line near Fleet. For reasons that are not reported, but probably cost was one consideration, it was not adopted by any of the three companies mentioned. See also https://www.railwaywondersof theworld.com/automatic-safety.html

Tony kindly adds a few pieces of additional information all reference *SW51*, 'Page 80, the E50xx electric loco displaying the 07 headcode is more than likely heading for Bricklayers Arms. Page 81 top, the unit has just crossed over from Down to Up Road for a return to Elmers End. There wasn't much juice rail beyond the bridge when the picture was taken! Headcode 3 applied in 1961 prior to changing to the more familiar 08. Page 81 bottom, the train is heading from Ramsgate to Victoria not vice versa. You can see a train in the Up Loop behind the waiting passengers.'

---

From **Colin Mason** of Chelsfield, but he adds 'formerly of Clapham Junction', and also on the subject of Graham Smith's EMU pictures in *SW51*. 'Graham Smith's EMU photos contain two comparative rarities at Clapham Junction: 4-LAV 2926 (p. 80) where the third vehicle is a 10-compartment suburban trailer 2nd, inserted in place of the corridor composite in 1963, presumably as the result of a mishap. Therefore, there are no toilet facilities in the unit, as these were only in the corridor coach. The different body profiles of the Bulleid and Maunsell designs are just discernible, as are the rainstrip arrangements.' Colin adds that the excellent David Brown book *Southern Electric – A New History* informs us that 4-LAV No. 2926 was the unit involved in the South Croydon collision on 24 October 1947, resulting in one Motor third brake (10511) being written off and replaced by a 2-HAL motor coach (10764 from unit No. 2646). The six-a-side SUB augmentation trailer third was No.10359 from 4-SUB 4338. In the surviving composite trailer the downgraded first class compartments were reinstated as partial recompense for the lost composite. In October 1967 a further revision saw a motor coach swap with unit No. 2941, all moves demonstrating the flexibility of Southern EMUs. 'There is an excellent photo of No. 2926 in its hybrid glory at Haywards Heath in 1965 by John Scrace on p. 97 of the book referred to.'

'4-RES 3067 (p. 78) is now a 4-COR(N): the dining 1st is retained but the restaurant 2nd has been replaced by a trailer 2nd from a disbanded 6-PUL. The second unit on the train is a 4-PUL, another 4-RES change, this time the restaurant car is replaced by a Pullman composite from a withdrawn 6-PUL.' (*If anyone would like to produce some further notes on the disbanding/reforming of EMU sets around this time we would be very interested – Ed.*)

'In issue 52 the photo of the Brighton radial on page 12 appears to show the smokebox door ajar – note the shadow and the obscuring of the smokebox front ring which should be clearly visible.' (*It does indeed, so why would an engine be running around, even within the confines of the depot, like this? The only answer has to be it was not securely fastened. But with SCT responsible for the image surely he would have noticed as well. Words may well have been said…. . – Ed.*)

'The Drummond 4-6-0 on page 88 (again *SW52*) is pictured heading west on the former Down fast approaching the west end of Clapham cutting, passing beneath the walls of Wandsworth prison, the nearer bridge being Heathfield Road, and visible through its arch, Trinity Road bridge. The period must be between the loco (T14 No.459) being built in June 1912 and the summer of 1915 (note the foliage), as the third, juice, rail for the Kingston roundabout service introduced on 30 January 1916 has yet to be installed. Incidentally the colourist has incorrectly coloured the dome and safety valve casings as brass, not green – an SECR season ticket holder perhaps?'

**The Edward Wallis image referred to by Jeremy Clarke, as it appeared in the late George Pryer's book.**

Next from **Jeremy Clarke**. 'Hi, Kevin…as second lockdown is now in operation I am taking advantage of being 'confined to barracks' to go through some back numbers knowing I'll come upon something I've missed first time around. So, *SW50* 'Rebuilt' p. 82, Nick Stanbury refers to the shunt signal pictured on p. 5 of *SW48*. This is a fitting unique (I think) to the LBSCR, being a working 'Limit of Shunt' signal: the 'L' means 'Limit'. A photograph of one at ground level appears on p. 59 of George Pryer's *A Pictorial Record of Southern Signals*, (OPC 1977), and I can do no better than quote from the caption. "… one of the more unusual features of the LB&SCR signalling was the provision of workable 'Limit of Shunt' signals. [The working] calls for some explanation. They were only to be found at locations where there were either two signal boxes, or a ground frame as well as a signal box. When one of [either] was not manned the limit of shunting movements was at the spot marked by such a signal. However, when [both] were open the limit could be extended under certain conditions as laid down in the special instructions for the place concerned." The face, by the way, is red but a green face with a white St George's cross on it is displayed when the signal is rotated through 90 degrees.' (*Fortunately an Edward Wallis image which we are able to reproduce courtesy of the family – Ed.*)

Now from **Eric Youldon** re the image of No. 857 with the enlarged boiler, *SW52* p.15 (see also accompanying image from Eric). 'LN Class locomotive No. 857 *Lord Howe* in black livery at Bournemouth West on 18 April 1943 with the special boiler No. 1063 refitted in the same year. Note that the smoke deflectors are now the standard Nelson pattern. Boiler No. 1063 was first fitted in January 1937 and removed in June 1941. When refitted in January 1943 it was accompanied by normal deflectors as confirmed by photographs until February 1945 when a standard boiler was provided. Boiler No. 1063 was discarded but lingered on the boiler dump at the rear of Eastleigh works until dispatched to Brighton for scrapping in January 1952. Why the deflectors were originally fitted with a crank in them is a mystery as the smokebox diameter of the special boiler was no greater than that of a standard Nelson.'

Eric also writes concerning the picture of the 'T14' Paddlebox on p. 88 of *SW52*. 'I once had, at a very early age, a soup plate lettered 'Baby's plate'. My mother knew what she

No. 857 *Lord Howe* at Bournemouth West in 1943 with straight deflectors but retaining the large boiler. Might the reason for the original angled deflectors have been a consideration as to visibility for the crew later found unnecessary? Similarly why was this large boiler not re-used on a different member of the class post-February 1945? *Eric Youldon collection*

was doing because food on the plate would be promptly cleared to reveal a Paddlebox picture. The only problem was the continual scraping by cutlery slowly eliminated the painting so it was nice to see it again in SW after more years than I care to remember.'

From **John Wenyon** concerning John Click's memories and the oil burning LMR 2-10-0 *Kitchener*. John comments, 'This beast came back to Eastleigh works in 1963/64 for overhaul having suffered a very nasty fire in the cab (broken pressure gauge glasses, etc). Eastleigh did its usual superb job on it but I recall that it had been fitted with a Laidlaw Drew swirly flow burner – was this the one from the Bulleid Pacific? Anyway it was John Click who fired it up for steam testing. Maybe that was indeed the final end of Southern oil firing steam locos?'

No. 601 *Kitchener* – incidentally the third Longmoor steam locomotive to have borne the name – as running as an oil burner post-1958. This engine also appeared in the film *The Great St Trinian's Train Robbery*, painted with supposed washable green paint on one side only. It subsequently transpired the paint could not be so easily removed and having later dropped a fusible plug, it ended its days a melancholy mixture of LMR blue and green and was scrapped.

Still on the subject of John Click's memories with this from **John Davenport**. 'As a train spotter I must have seen some of the earlier runs (35005) which left a wonderful smoke trail, never mind the flying objects: it was more like a Dreadnought laying down a smoke-screen. Later that expert, Inspector Plummer, was my footplate companion when I had a footplate pass for the 'ACE' on the 80 minute Waterloo – Salisbury schedule. I have a photo of him sitting on the fireman's seat looking forwards and completely relaxed….. . A correction now, p. 78 **(***SW52***)** the ROC medal was for 12 years' service (I've got one) but no mention of good conduct! (John included a slightly fuzzy image of the moment the Corps Commandant 'pulled the chain' *(meaning pulled the string to open the curtain),* … us unofficial 'Erks' were parked well away to the side.' John continues, 'Enough waffle…. .' *(No never, please keep it coming! – Ed.)*

---

Next from **Tony Francis,** and *SW50* which as with the preceding submissions goes to prove there is still new information out there. 'In Issue 50 there are references to 'Larman' and 'Larry L'. I'm putting two and two together and assuming that this is Larry Larman.'

'In 1979 I wanted to move on from my job as a rolling-stock fitter at Gillingham and applied for a post in the CM&EE Drawing Office at Southern House, Croydon. Larry interviewed me and I received a grilling on bogies, their components and purpose. Luckily I was successful and commenced as a Technical Officer. I didn't talk to Larry very often about things not currently to do with work in the office but on one occasion for some reason the subject of the 'River' class tanks came up. Larry startled me by saying he had a nameplate off one of the class in his garage. Naturally I asked him which one and he nonchalantly said he couldn't remember. I've never seen any references to the River plates surviving so to this day I wonder if it's true and what happened to it.'

'The Drawing Office at Croydon was never envisaged to exist, with all technical staff moving to the Technical Centre at Derby when the Drawing Office at Brighton closed. However, an 11th hour change of mind led to a few staff moving to Croydon. Among the Draughtsmen I worked with who came from Brighton were Larry, Norman Dunster and Stuart Benson. Norman is the one who had done the General Arrangement drawing for the Leader, indeed some diagrams have the initials NSD in the 'drawn by' box. He was also involved with the Standard 4 tanks and worked on the tanks themselves. He told me that one Saturday they carried out a test in Brighton Works to test the actual tank water capacity compared to the design estimate.'

'Two years later I moved to the Divisional Traction Engineer's office in Essex House, Croydon, and met Ken Briggs who had worked in the Testing Section at Brighton so must have worked with John Click. Ken told me that he worked with the Leader and one of the jobs he was given was to observe the behaviour of the valve gear. This was 40 years ago but I'm convinced that he told me that it involved riding in a box between the bogies. He never elaborated as to whether this was with the loco out of steam and towed around the works yard or in steam!'

'Another one in there was Bill Brophy, now from the Bluebell Railway. He was in the office longer than me so he might have chatted to Norman Dunster about Brighton Works days – their drawing boards were next to one another.

'On a completely unrelated matter, Ken Briggs lived in Hailsham so got a train to Polegate and thence to Brighton. He wanted a base for his garden shed so asked the local P. Way supervisor if he had any old sleepers no longer required. The supervisor said he would sort something out and no more was said. A few weeks later Ken got off his train at Hailsham and one of the Porters said 'Mr Briggs?' Ken answered in the affirmative. The Porter then said, 'There's a wagon in the yard with your sleepers in it.' The P. Way Supervisor at Brighton must have identified some sleepers, arranged for them to be loaded and then tripped from Brighton to Hailsham!'

---

Still on the topic of *SW52* and from **Roger Whitehouse**. 'Chris Heaps' charter of the VSOE was not its first visit to the Mid-Sussex. On Saturday 16 April 1983 the RCTS chartered the set for a railtour whose title I failed to note in my records. *(The 'Six Bells' website simply has it recorded as 'RCTS VSOE Pullman Tour' – Ed.)* Departing from the Chatham side at Victoria, we went via Stewarts Lane to Pouparts Junction then Dorking and the Mid-Sussex to Chichester where the train shunted out of the way of some ordinary service trains. Then direct to Fareham, and via Eastleigh to a stop on the Laverstock loop.'

'The locos were EDLs 73 142 *Broadlands* and 73 129 *City of Winchester*. The Cars were *Minerva, Ione, Zena, Cygnus, Perseus, Audrey,* and *Phoenix,* tailed by Baggage Cars 9 & 7. Unfortunately, despite extensive testing on the previous day, the second EDL failed to contribute on diesel power, so we embarked on the climb to Grateley with just 500hp. After a brief stop at Basingstoke (I believe to summon technical assistance to Clapham Junction) we were going like the wind from Hook!

'Our route back was via Chertsey, Staines and (I think) Hounslow to Clapham Junction, then Kensington Olympia to reverse, returning to Victoria with the train in the right order for its next trip.'

---

Penultimately, from **Anthony Andrews** on *SW50.* 'Having only recently got my copy of *SW50*, at a visit to the Bluebell, I have just seen the picture on page 7.

'In answer to your question it is not Brighton but actually Strood. You are looking South with the road going to join Rochester Bridge or Strood High Street to the right. The lines to the left were stock sidings with the Maidstone West line nearest. The L1 is on a Down working and about to enter the site of Rochester Bridge Station before passing where Toomers Loop comes up (out of sight to the left) and joins the main line before crossing the Medway and on to Rochester and the coast. In the sidings, the unit is a 2-HAL, introduced for the Gillingham electrification and awaiting its next turn from Strood on the North Kent to London. The L1 looks to be 31753 or 31755, which would be one of the trio shedded at Gillingham around the middle-50s.

'Hope this is not too much detail, but it is nice to see a previously unseen view from my home area. No doubt you will remember the war memorial photo from Gillingham Station that graced an early edition of *SW* that I found in my father's pictures. The Medway is generally under exposed in Southern publishing, so please can we have more.

'Having seen the great picture of Gillingham on p. 78, although the building is actually the former one from New Brompton, from which my grandfather moved the booking office to the new station on the overbridge when it opened in the late 1930s, no doubt with my father helping (or hindering), before being put on the footplate of a 'Schools' or 'Arthur' with instructions to 'put him off' at Bromley South so not to be spotted by authority at Victoria. A homecoming on the cushions followed before returning home to Sunday Lunch. The HAP pairing is quite interesting as I had always thought that the internal Corridor units were confined to the western section. I may come back after some further research.

'What really raised the eyebrows was the picture above. What a rare unnoticed gem. A trio of Nelsons including a Pullman. This dates the picture to between 1969 and 1973. Following the introduction of the 4-BIG & CIGs on the Brighton line, a number of the redundant 6-PUL units had the Pullman removed and the resulting five-car units were paired and used on the Eastern for the Ramsgate to Cannon Street business services. Some of the composite Pullman cars then found their way into 4-RES and BUF units such as seen here. Overall though a grand set of pictures. Hopefully there are more to come.' *(We do intend more EMU images soon. Similarly, although Anthony's letter may be slightly later than others in responding to the location which we could not at first identify, it was well worth including due to the local knowledge Anthony was able to impart – Ed.)*

Anthony then came back with a bit more on the 4-COR picture. 'It is actually a bit earlier than I thought – being mid-60s – when some of these reformed 4-RES units with 4-CORs were used as part of the changeover to BR designed units on the Brighton Line. Therefore, to respectfully correct your caption, the 16 does not represent a Guildford working, but actually a Victoria to Littlehampton service. Sorry to have done this piecemeal but at least the correct answer emerges... .'

---

Finally **Neil Knowldon** adds some detail and comments re *SW51*.

'p. 5: Though it's a pull-push set complete with air-control pram-van, the M7 doesn't have the appropriate fitting so will have to run round at Brockenhurst.

'p. 31: Set 4342 has been reduced to motor coaches only and is obviously eking out its last days as depot tractor.

'p. 50/51: You mention that 80043 was built at Brighton ... but 48706 was too!

'p. 78: Not only a 4-RES but a 4-PUL too – the business gentlemen of Guildford won't be going hungry on this train.

**Probably a Victoria to Eastbourne service arriving at the latter terminus. The set is a 6-PUL including the Pullman car *Iris*.**

The companion view to that seen on page 47, No. 30034 still engaged in pilot duties at Salisbury with some cold looking Bulleid coaches alongside.

'p. 81: While this is obviously the off-peak electric shuttle from Elmers End – returning to the station after crossing over – the ten-car-stop board might be more wishful thinking than peak-hour fact: whatever ran through from Charing Cross/Cannon Street probably never had more than a handful of passengers south of Woodside. (Interesting to see the tail lamp (still) in place as the use of red tail blinds would have been normal: maybe a local regulation as the crew couldn't change ends once they were beyond the platform?) The nine-car-stop board would have applied to Uckfield/East Grinstead 'thumpers', of course.

'p. 101: From what I can piece together, there were two of these 5-TCB sets created as stop-gap – not only has the 'host' 4-TC gained a REP Buffet Car but – in this case – the REP Trailer Brake First, too. From the 1989 Platform 5 'Combo' I reckon this is set 2807: one time 4-TC 433 (Driving Trailers 76945/6) with Trailer First 70854 from 4-TC 411 and Trailer Buffet 69022 + Trailer Brake First 71156 from 4-REP 3012 … but there were so many temporary re-formations, that could be totally wrong!'

**Next time in the July issue of *The Southern Way* (issue 55), we start a major article by Richard Simmons on Christmas and Parcels traffic (yes, we do know it is July!), Mike King's *'Down to Earth'* series continues with Part 4 on grounded bodies of former SECR stock, plus the Railways of Dulwich, Buriton chalk pits, S. C. Townroe in colour of course, and at least one photo feature.**

Stored engines – later days. The scene at Templecombe 1965/6. Modern motive power at a standstill, possible not as well maintained as it might have been, but only redundant as the services they used to operate are now withdrawn.

The Raynes Park Derailment

Feltham's crane disposes of a long wheelbase utility van and places it in the cess beside the Up Local line.

As a Class 1 train, it was ordinarily allowed to run at up to 75mph, but was still in the 60mph limit for all lines in the inner London suburban area. Due to a shortage of more suitable vehicles, however, the train of vans contained seven fitted vehicles each with a wheelbase of only 10 feet and hence restricted to a maximum speed of 45mph, a fact they had guard failed to communicate to the driver before leaving Waterloo.

Due to the staggered nature of the platform layout of Raynes Park station, the support and staircase of the steel girder footbridge, spanning the four main lines on a skew, are at the very London end of the Down platform, which meant that the columns took the full brunt of the impact from the colliding derailed van. The three vertical rolled steel sections forming the support at that the end of the footbridge span were bent and distorted to such an extent that they were torn away from their holding-down bolts in the concrete base slab. Although still standing, they could not, therefore, be relied upon to support the load, especially if subjected to vibration from passing trains. So, once the debris in the immediate vicinity was cleared away, staff of the District Engineer's Building Section, who fortunately were based in the goods yard at Raynes Park, were quickly on the scene to erect timber props in the Down Local to secure the structure. This enabled the DE's Steelworks Section from Wimbledon, just down the road, to cut away the damaged steelwork and to erect more permanent support clear of the tracks. Subsequently it carried out permanent repairs.

The breakdown trains from Wimbledon Park and Feltham were summoned to clear the line, using their 75-ton and 30-ton Cowans Sheldon diesel cranes, Nos. DB965186 and DB965183 working on the Up Through line to lift heavier items and place them beyond the Up Local line to be cleared away later. Concurrently members of the Permanent Way staff were attending to the damaged track-work as it was cleared.

Although the Up Branch remained useable throughout, there was little point when trains could not return; so, it was 14.36 before traffic was restored in both directions to and from Motspur Park and beyond to Epsom and Chessington. Running on the Up Main Local was resumed from 15.35 and the two Main Through lines from 16.45, but the Down Main Local was not made available until 05.42 the next morning.

Ref: *Report on the derailment that occurred on 28th November 1967 at Raynes Park in the Southern Region British Railways*, Ministry of Transport, HMSO, 1968.

**Likewise the wheels of the Vanfit are swung away by Feltham's crane.**

**The offending Vanfit being lifted by Feltham's 30-ton crane No. DB965183.**

Luckily for the guard, he was travelling in another guard's van further forward in the train, because this is all that was left of a 20-ton goods brake van.

*All views by the Author*

# The Long Lost Shirley Holms Halt

## Roger Simmonds

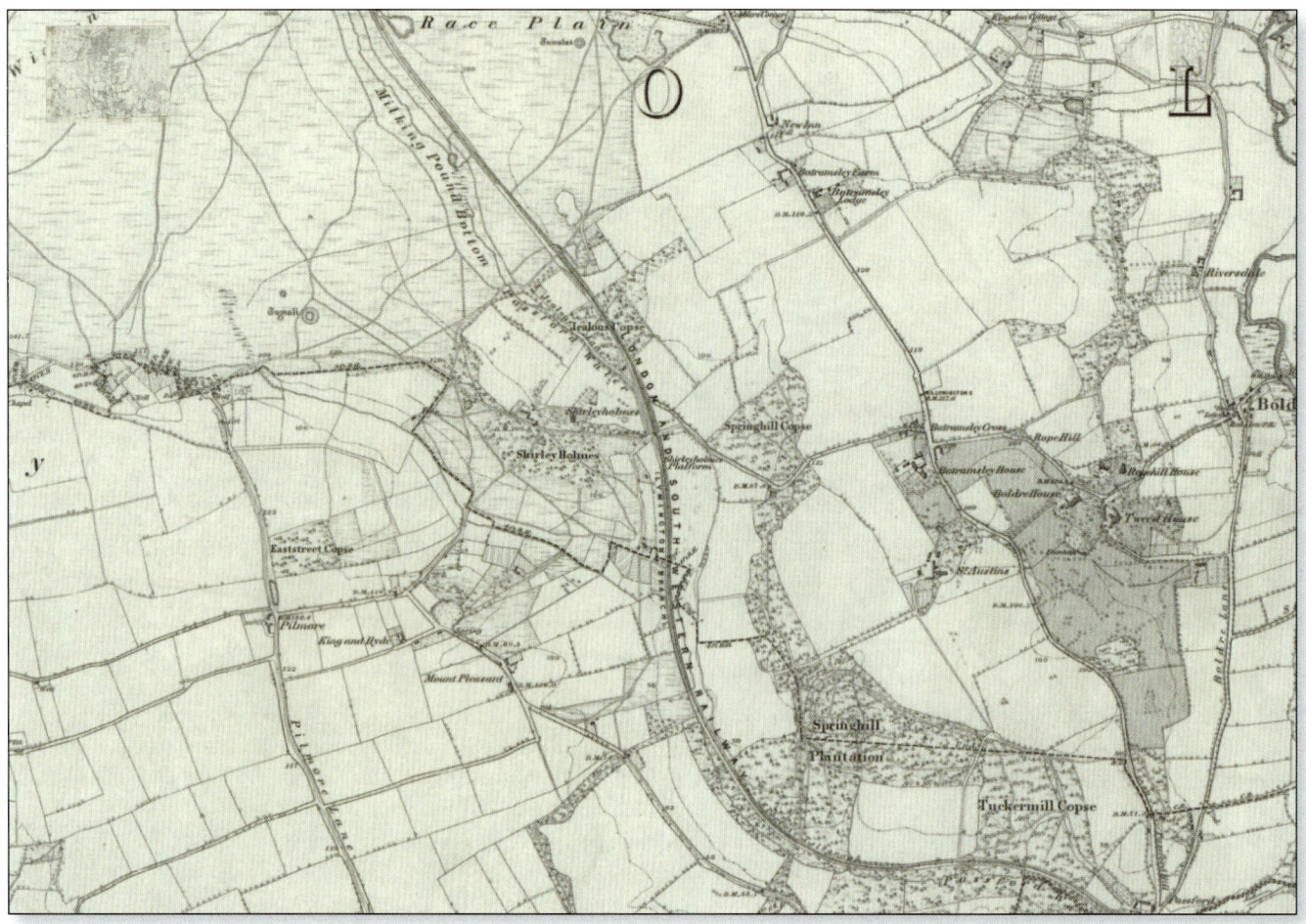

1871 OS Map giving their location of the stopping place; shown on the west side of the branch. *Courtesy OS*

Shirley Holmes (later spelt Holms) is one of those places that elicits the usual answer of *"where the heck is that?"* or even *"who was she?"*. A further fact that it once had a station (albeit primitive) further puzzles the responder. Well it did exist and it is believed to have been one of the first stations in the UK referred to formally as a Halt as we know it today. Its obscurity is hardly surprising as it only existed for a mere 28 years before closing and being forgotten.

So where was it, why did it exist, and what was its origins? It effectively was just a simple wooden platform located on the Lymington branch in Hampshire, to be precise about a mile south of Lymington Junction where the LSWR main line carried on west to Dorchester and the branch curved away due south. Anyone would be hard pressed to find any remains today, but if you know where to look a short grassy mound of earth marks the spot.

A branch line from Brockenhurst to Lymington was first mooted in 1844 as plans for the Southampton & Dorchester Railway were progressing. This line opened throughout on 1 June 1847. An early proposal to site a station called Latchmoor at what would be Lymington Junction was changed and re-sited at what is now Brockenhurst. The good folks of Lymington were frustrated as parliamentary approval for a line to the town was delayed through a dithering London & South Western Railway who had absorbed the Southampton & Dorchester but final sanction for the line was given in 1856 and an Act for construction was passed on 7 July. Following the Board of Trade inspection on 11 May 1858, the railway was officially opened to the public on 12 July 1858, the short delay being caused by the LSWR requiring some changes to the permanent way.

# The Long Lost Shirley Holms Halt

|  | LYMINGTON RAILWAY. | | | | | | | | | | | | |
|---|---|---|---|---|---|---|---|---|---|---|---|---|---|
| Miles. | TRAINS FROM LYMINGTON TO BROCKENHURST. | | | | | | | | | | | | |
| | STATIONS. | WEEK DAYS. | | | | | | | Empty | SUNDAYS. | | | |
| | | a.m. | a.m. | a.m. | a.m. | p.m. | p.m. | p.m. | p.m. | p.m. | a.m. | p.m. | p.m. |
| 5¼ | Lymington ........... dep. | 6 25 | 7 50 | 10 10 | 11 0 | 1 40 | 2 15 | 5 40 | 6 25 | 7 45 | 7 45 | 1 10 | 4 5 |
| | Brockenhurst ........ arr. | 6 40 | 8 0 | 10 25 | 11 12 | 1 50 | 2 25 | 5 55 | 6 40 | 8 0 | 8 0 | 2 25 | 4 20 |
| | TRAINS FROM BROCKENHURST TO LYMINGTON. | | | | | | | | | | | | |
| | STATIONS. | WEEK DAYS. | | | | | | | | | SUNDAYS | | |
| | | a.m. | a.m. | a.m. | a.m. | p.m. | p.m. | p.m. | p.m. | p.m. | a.m. | p.m. | p.m. |
| 5¼ | Brockenhurst ........ dep. | 6 50 | 8 20 | 10 34 | 11 20 | 2 0 | 2 30 | 6 0 | 6 45 | 8 10 | 8 30 | 2 37 | 4 30 |
| | Lymington ........... arr. | 7 5 | 8 30 | 10 45 | 11 30 | 2 10 | 2 40 | 6 15 | 7 0 | 8 25 | 8 45 | 2 52 | 4 45 |

Enginemen in charge of Trains on the Dorchester Line, must approach the Junction near to Brockenhurst Station with great caution, and at such a rate of speed, that their Trains can be quickly stopped if necessary.

Slightly earlier, the working timetable page for services on the branch from 1861. Shirley Holms is not shown; neither are separate goods trains.

And so, to Shirley Holmes (sic). The Lymington Railway Company was of course worked by the LSWR, and it was suggested by the LRC Directors at a half-yearly meeting in 1860 that a station be provided to serve the not far away villages of Sway and Boulder (remember the route through Sway to Bournemouth had not been built at the time). Shirley Holmes itself was little more than a tiny hamlet consisting of a handful of cottages all situated along one single street, in this regard making it fairly unique in the UK. Its only other notable feature was a late bronze age bowl barrow located close to an area known as Milking Pound Bottom.

With the agreement of the LSWR plans were set in motion to erect a station close to Springhill Copse and to the east of these few dwelling places of Shirley Holmes. For whatever reason, the original scheme, which included station buildings, was scaled down significantly and what was eventually opened on 10 October 1860 was a simple wooden platform with no other facilities or even lighting. As seen on the 1871 map, the station known as Shirley Holmes Platform was later referred to as Shirley Holmes Halt. It was located on the west side of the line by the underbridge on a slight right-hand curve.

Operationally it served during daylight hours only and would-be passengers from Lymington wishing to alight had to inform the guard. Anyone wishing to join the train at Shirley Holmes had to hand signal to the driver. Passengers in the down direction had to inform the guard at Brockenhurst.

Official records include a notice issued at the time of opening. *"Shirley Holmes Station – On and after Wednesday 10 October all trains running between Lymington and Brockenhurst will stop at that platform on the up journey to take up passengers and on the down journey to set down passengers. On the up journey the trains will not stop after daylight. Passengers for up trains must be waiting on the platform before trains approach, otherwise the trains will not stop. Passengers by down trains must inform the guard of the Lymington train when they desire to be put down at the platform. By the down trains passengers must have tickets for Lymington. By the up trains passengers must take tickets at Brockenhurst paying in addition the fare from Lymington".*

Ticketing was therefore not exactly encouraging patronage, and indeed publicity fell short too as the Halt was not even mentioned in the LSWR public timetables! It is impossible to ascertain how many passengers utilised the Halt during its short life as no records exist and no tickets were printed with the name of the station as a destination. Equally, it was never photographed by any early enthusiasts or travellers. Its obscurity makes it more interesting in many ways, and who knows what might come to light in the future however unlikely.

The death nell for what was probably a little used Halt inevitably came about when the Bournemouth direct route was opened on 5 March 1888, Sway now had its own station and after a short time Shirley Holmes was consigned to history and largely forgotten.

Up P + P branch train arriving at Lymington Junction.

P + P train on the branch and close to the site of the stopping place, 4 May 1958 and some 70 years after Shirley Holms had ceased to exist.
*Tony Molyneaux*

# A Very Brief Visit to Newhaven – June 1952

## Courtesy Gerry Nichols and the Stephenson Locomotive Society

Comparisons at Newhaven. On 16 June 1942 Bruce Natham recorded three totally different modes of transport at Newhaven. Seen first is E4 0-6-2T No. 32504 on freight, interestingly the engine sports a painted rather than a coast front number.

*Opposite top:* **This was followed by a 'Hornby'; more accurately the BR version, No. 20003 on a boat train working.**

*Bottom:* **Finally perhaps the most interesting of the trio in those pre-'drive-on' days. 'Have crane will travel'!**

# Architecture and Imagery on the Cuckoo Line

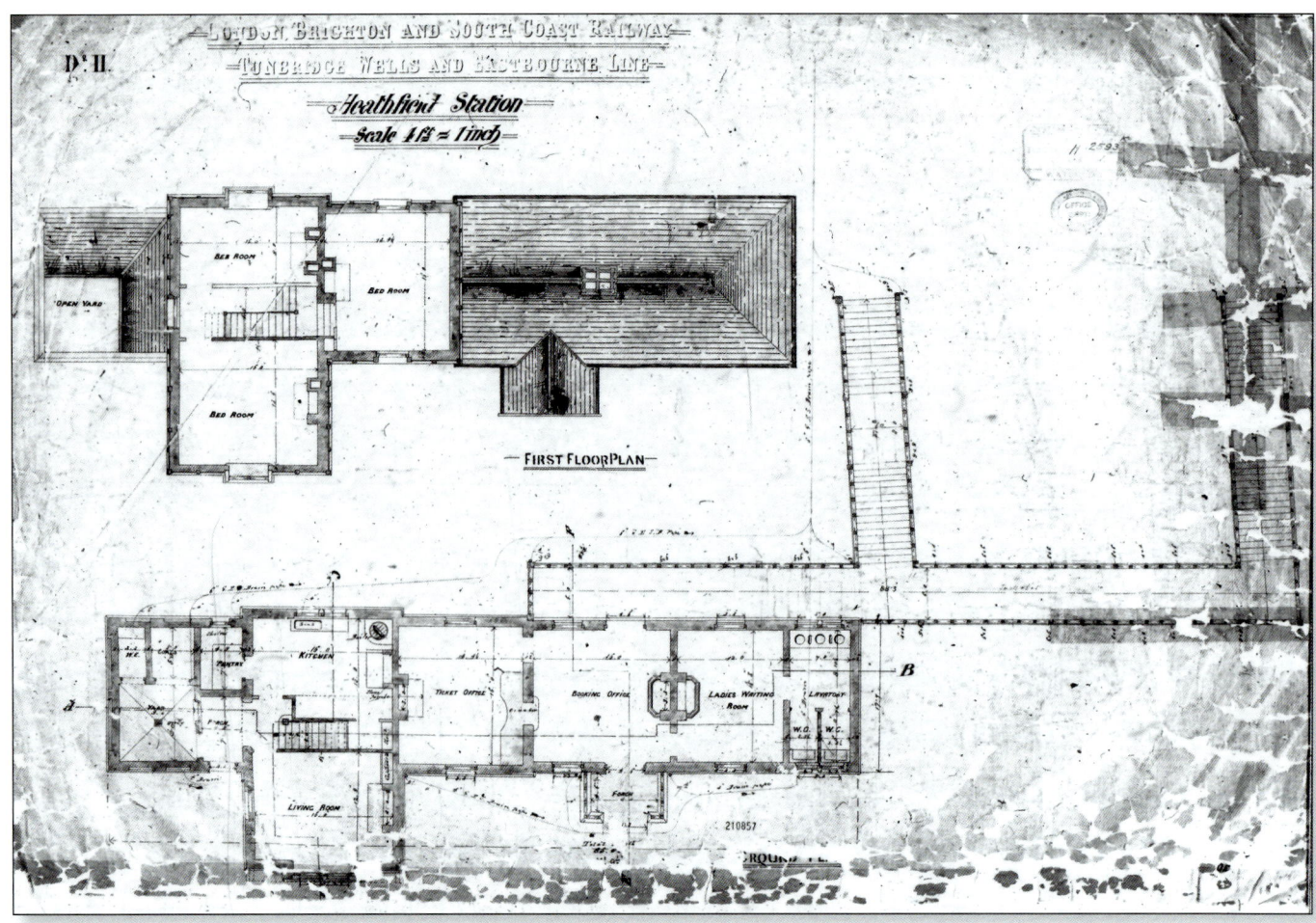

Thanks to the endeavours of David Lawrence, we have been fortunate to recently been given access to four architectural plans of Heathfield station. Add this to another from the archives of Graham Smith and the results speak for themselves.

# Architecture and Imagery on the Cuckoo Line

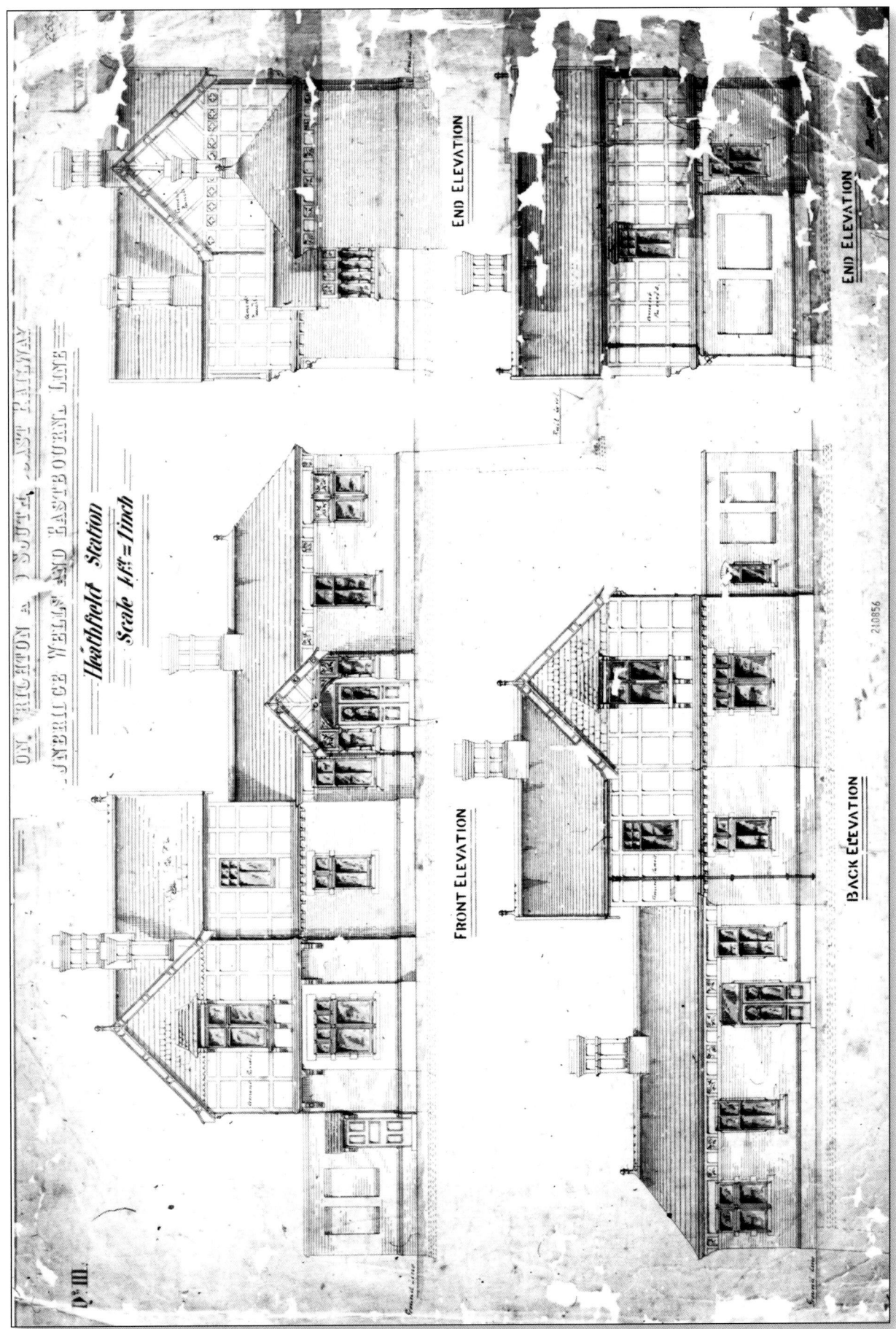

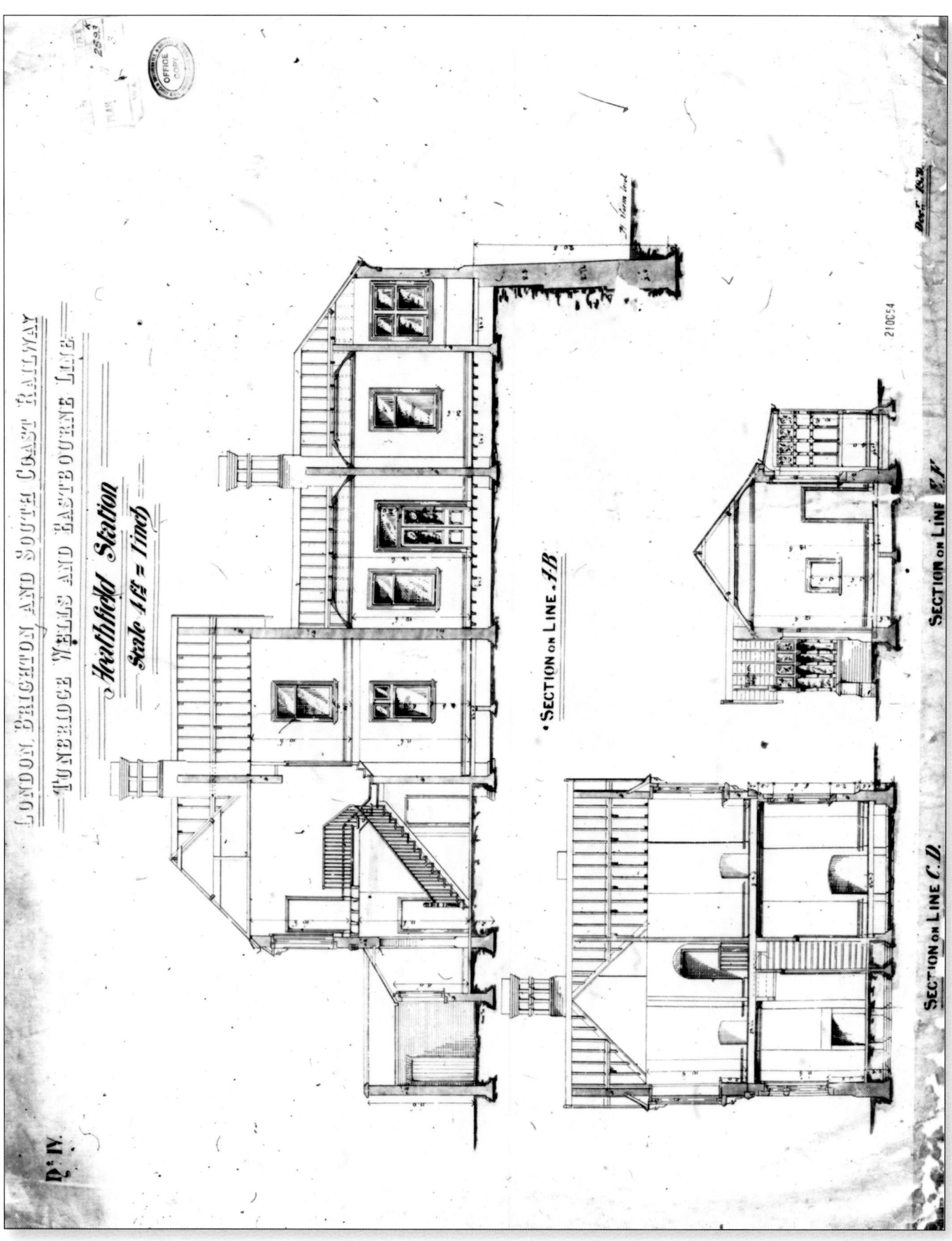

# Architecture and Imagery on the Cuckoo Line

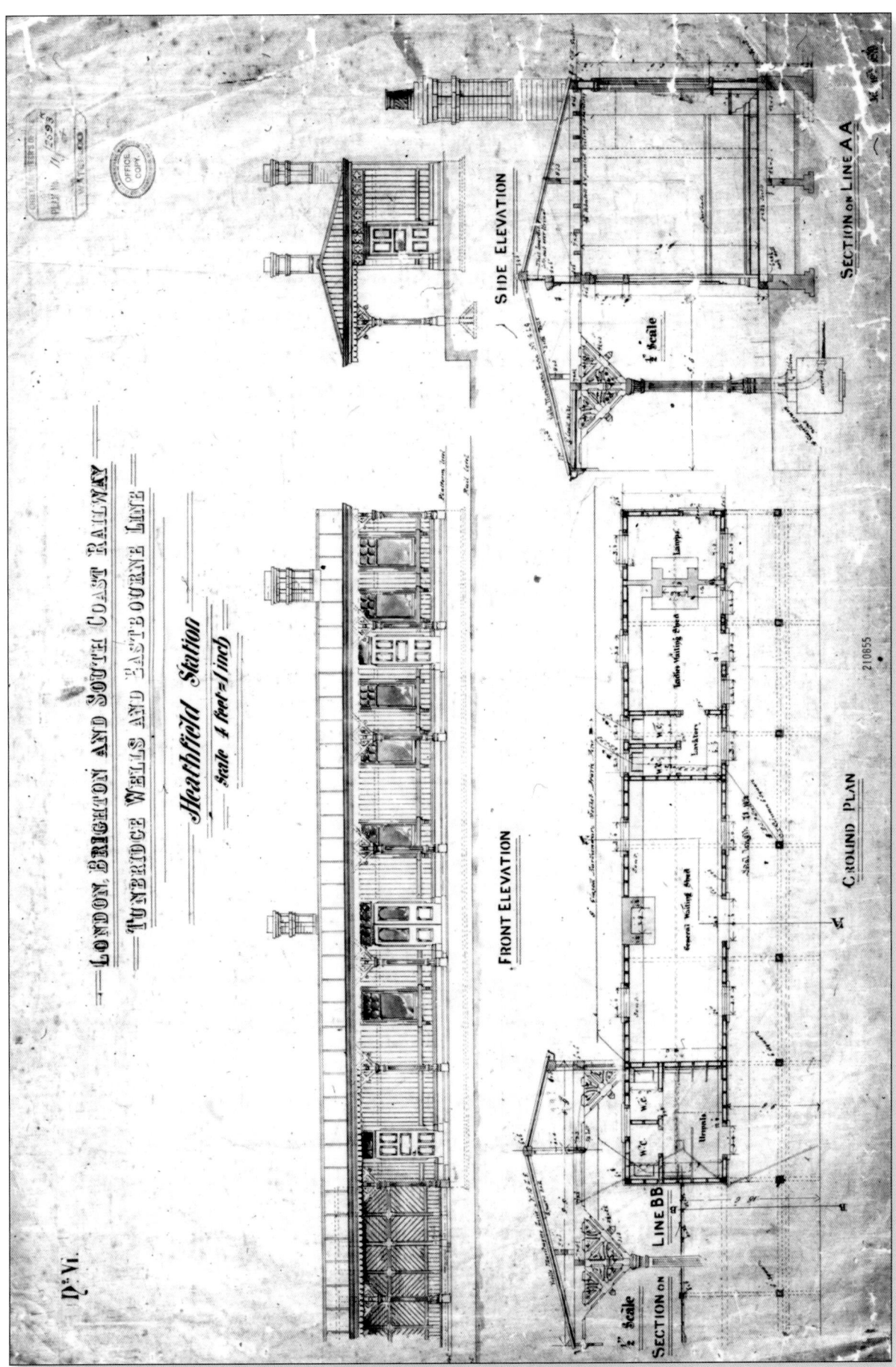

**Heathfield from track level and north towards Mayfield. Architecturally the station remained basically unaltered throughout its 80 year lifespan – although the VHF television on the chimney is certainly not original! There is a distinct lack of obvious traffic; a line of empty 4-wheel trolleys but not even a single parcel visible. Hopefully the goods yard (now an industrial estate was somewhat more profitable). Whilst at rail level the site has been cleared the station house and former booking office remain.** *Graham Smith*

# Architecture and Imagery on the Cuckoo Line

**Undated but early view of Heathfield looking back towards the main station and with the split level buddings visible on the road above. (More detail on the 'Cuckoo Line' will be found in the Crécy paperback on the route.)**

# Looking Back...

The LSWR Exeter – Chagford road motor possibly soon after its introduction. We should not take the advertisement on the roofboard too literally as this was meant to refer to the railway and not the road service!

We recently re-discovered a large box of prints and negatives given to us some years ago and which had regretfully been hidden under other items for some time. Apart from the SR and constituents, there was also material from the LMS, GER, NER and even the GW; all of these have of course been omitted! A quick dusting and a warming up of the scanner produced the following results. Very little in the way of caption information, but we hope a few items of interest from days past – as found and so deliberately not in specific order.

Looking Back...

There was, indeed is, something about the light railways operated by Col. Stephens, this is just one example; the Hundred of Manhood & Selsey Tramway. We don't think we have used this one previously and it shows the scene at Selsey Town more than a century ago. Light rail in the literal sense.

Speaking of architecture, we have here Shoreham (by Sea) supposedly even earlier in the 1870s. The costume would certainly appear to be correct as indeed would be ballast covered sleepers, possibly the station master (agent) with his family on the right hand side.

Still in roughly the same area – well the Coast line at least – this is Emsworth west of Chichester. The neat canopy valancing is so typical of the LBSCR whilst in the siding the sheeted wagons raise questions as to their contents. We may consider todays 21st century railway stations (I refuse to say 'train station') are little more than an opportunity for commerce, but note here the same situation existed years past. The tall starting signal would provide a reasonable view of its position for an approaching train.

Still at Emsworth and still with a sheeted wagon in the siding. Slightly unusual in that the illustration is devoid of people; even the loco crew are elsewhere.

At Worthing the use of a hipped and glazed canopy added much to the brightness of the platforms making the whole more akin the architecture of a church or even cathedral; perhaps fortunately the railway did not go further and add stained glass!

West Croydon exterior, functional yet austere, the canopy valance giving the latter an almost heavy appearance. Southern Railway bill-boards dominate.

Closer to London now at Purley. Impressive with its platform layout – was the timber section due to weight constraints underneath? Another image without any people so deliberately posed perhaps?

This one just had to be included because of those signals (and the telegraph pole opposite) – and no, it is not an Edward Wallis view. We are told it is a an Eridge train.

Another mystery, no location but we believe Croydon area and from the serviceman possibly WW1. The sacking 'Dog Cakes' is delightful.

To the concourse at London Bridge (note the seatback) with some wonderful contemporary advertising. Again who says commerce is a new thing, the railway companies seeing such opportunities as a means of gaining extra revenue.

The approaches to London Bridge some years before the present layout and seen from Borough Market Junction.

# Errata
## In More Ways Than One!

Two 'erratas'; one by the full size railway – and one by us. Firstly the loco. Seen outside the front of Eastleigh shed is Stanier 2-8-0 identified as No. 90734. It is the former WD No. 70320 which became WD 501 in 1952. Eastleigh were tasked with a renumbering, but it got it wrong – twice; first 90743 and then corrected to that seen here – 90734, both engines in the Riddles WD 2-8-0 series. What should have been allocated is No. 48774 famed now as preserved (with this correct LMR number) on the Severn Valley Railway.

Errata No. 2. John Davenport was quick to point out that in SW53 the gremlins had been at work. The caption on p67 should have been 'An unusual chain-operated centre-pivot bi-directional signal at Herne Hill sidings. The signal applied to movements in either direction and was of necessitate both an upper and lower quadrant – dependent upon direction of travel. Notice the lamp below the arm. On both sides this had a red glass to cover the white lamp and so show 'stop' when the arm was horizontal. When the arm was cleared a white light was displayed.' To make matters worse we also invented a new work on p89. 'bowevereing' – I think the dictionary definition should be 'to have a senior moment'. Sincere apologies.

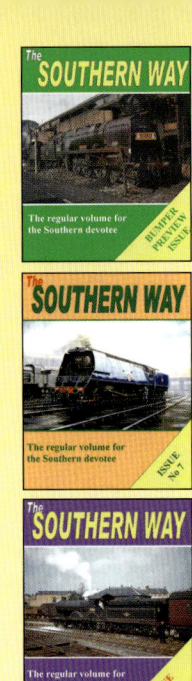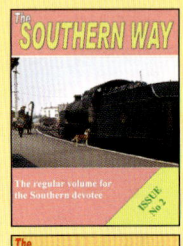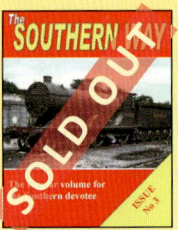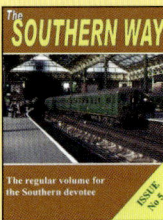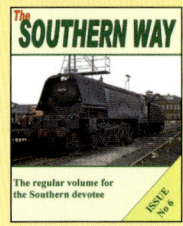
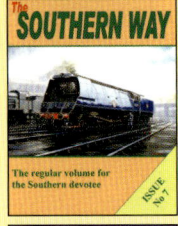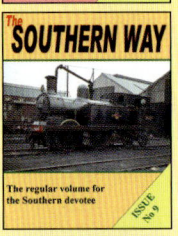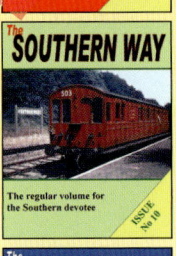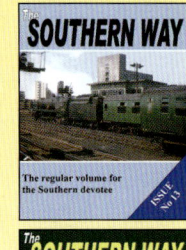
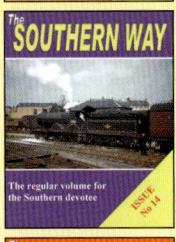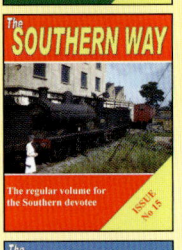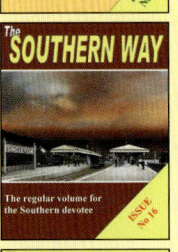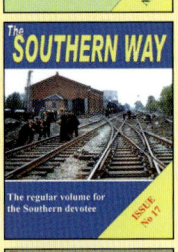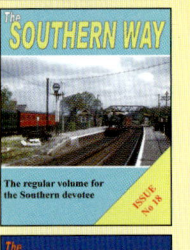
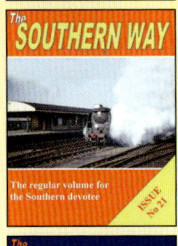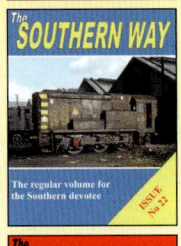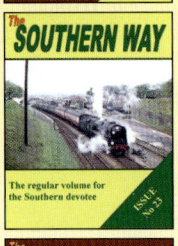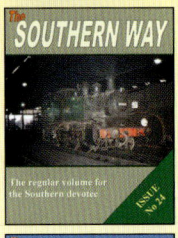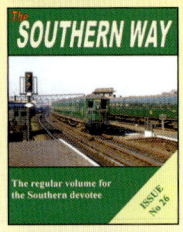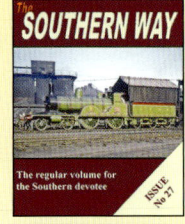
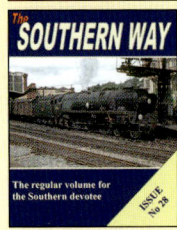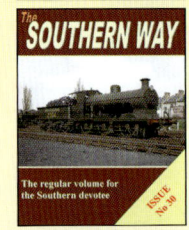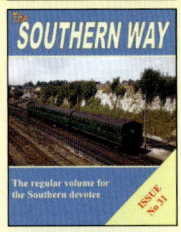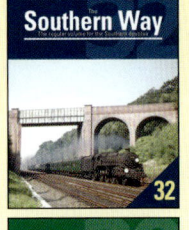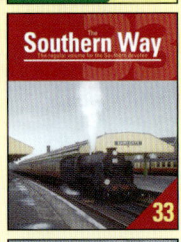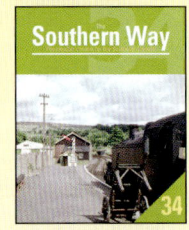
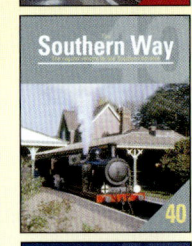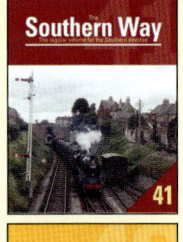
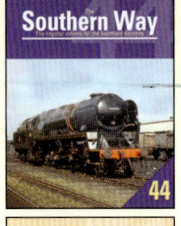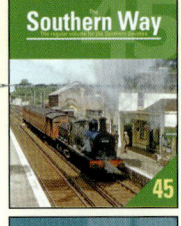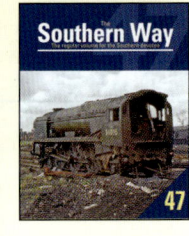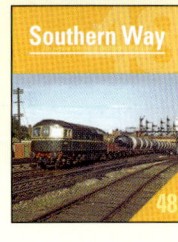
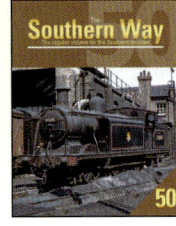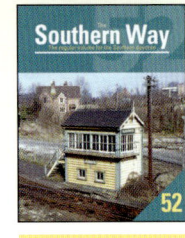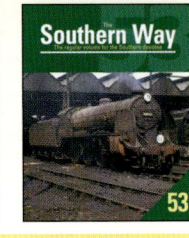

# The Southern Way
The regular volume for the Southern devotee
**MOST RECENT BACK ISSUES**

*The Southern Way* is available from all good book sellers, or in case of difficulty, direct from the publisher. (Post free UK) Each regular issue contains at least 96 pages including colour content.

£11.95 each
£12.95 from Issue 7
£14.50 from Issue 21
£14.95 from Issue 35

Subscription for four-issues available (Post free in the UK)
www.crecy.co.uk